Teach Yourself
VISUALLY™
iPhoto® '09

Visual

by Lonzell Watson

WILEY

Wiley Publishing, Inc.

Teach Yourself VISUALLY™ iPhoto® '09

Published by
Wiley Publishing, Inc.
10475 Crosspoint Boulevard
Indianapolis, IN 46256
www.wiley.com

Published simultaneously in Canada

Library of Congress Control Number: 2009929463

ISBN: 978-0-470-48193-6

Manufactured in the United States of America

10 9 8 7 6 5 4 3 2 1

Trademark Acknowledgments

Contact Us

For general information on our other products and services please contact our Customer Care Department within the U.S. at 877-762-2974, outside the U.S. at 317-572-3993 or fax 317-572-4002.

For technical support please visit www.wiley.com/techsupport.

Wiley Publishing, Inc.

Sales

Contact Wiley
at (877) 762-2974 or
fax (317) 572-4002.

Praise for Visual Books

"Like a lot of other people, I understand things best when I see them visually. Your books really make learning easy and life more fun."

John T. Frey (Cadillac, MI)

"I have quite a few of your Visual books and have been very pleased with all of them. I love the way the lessons are presented!"

Mary Jane Newman (Yorba Linda, CA)

"I just purchased my third Visual book (my first two are dog-eared now!), and, once again, your product has surpassed my expectations.

Tracey Moore (Memphis, TN)

"I am an avid fan of your Visual books. If I need to learn anything, I just buy one of your books and learn the topic in no time. Wonders! I have even trained my friends to give me Visual books as gifts."

Illona Bergstrom (Aventura, FL)

"Thank you for making it so clear. I appreciate it. I will buy many more Visual books."

J.P. Sangdong (North York, Ontario, Canada)

"I have several books from the Visual series and have always found them to be valuable resources."

Stephen P. Miller (Ballston Spa, NY)

"Thank you for the wonderful books you produce. It wasn't until I was an adult that I discovered how I learn — visually. Nothing compares to Visual books. I love the simple layout. I can just grab a book and use it at my computer, lesson by lesson. And I understand the material! You really know the way I think and learn. Thanks so much!"

Stacey Han (Avondale, AZ)

"I absolutely admire your company's work. Your books are terrific. The format is perfect, especially for visual learners like me. Keep them coming!"

Frederick A. Taylor, Jr. (New Port Richey, FL)

"I have several of your Visual books and they are the best I have ever used."

Stanley Clark (Crawfordville, FL)

"I bought my first Teach Yourself VISUALLY book last month. Wow. Now I want to learn everything in this easy format!"

Tom Vial (New York, NY)

"Thank you, thank you, thank you...for making it so easy for me to break into this high-tech world. I now own four of your books. I recommend them to anyone who is a beginner like myself."

Gay O'Donnell (Calgary, Alberta, Canada)

"I write to extend my thanks and appreciation for your books. They are clear, easy to follow, and straight to the point. Keep up the good work! I bought several of your books and they are just right! No regrets! I will always buy your books because they are the best."

Seward Kollie (Dakar, Senegal)

"Compliments to the chef!! Your books are extraordinary! Or, simply put, extra-ordinary, meaning way above the rest! THANK YOU THANK YOU THANK YOU! I buy them for friends, family, and colleagues."

Christine J. Manfrin (Castle Rock, CO)

"What fantastic teaching books you have produced! Congratulations to you and your staff. You deserve the Nobel Prize in Education in the Software category. Thanks for helping me understand computers."

Bruno Tonon (Melbourne, Australia)

"Over time, I have bought a number of your 'Read Less - Learn More' books. For me, they are THE way to learn anything easily. I learn easiest using your method of teaching."

José A. Mazón (Cuba, NY)

"I am an avid purchaser and reader of the Visual series, and they are the greatest computer books I've seen. The Visual books are perfect for people like myself who enjoy the computer, but want to know how to use it more efficiently. Your books have definitely given me a greater understanding of my computer, and have taught me to use it more effectively. Thank you very much for the hard work, effort, and dedication that you put into this series."

Alex Diaz (Las Vegas, NV)

Credits

Senior Acquisitions Editor
Jody Lefevere

Project Editor
Jade L. Williams

Technical Editor
Dennis Cohen

Copy Editor
Scott Tullis

Editorial Director
Robyn Siesky

Editorial Manager
Cricket Krengel

Business Manager
Amy Knies

Senior Marketing Manager
Sandy Smith

Vice President and Executive Group Publisher
Richard Swadley

Vice President and Executive Publisher
Barry Pruett

Project Coordinator
Katherine Crocker

Graphics and Production Specialists
Carrie A. Cesavice
Joyce Haughey
Andrea Hornberger
Jennifer Mayberry
Mark Pinto

Quality Control Technician
Melissa Cossell

Proofreading and Indexing
Debbye Butler
BIM Indexing &
Proofreading Services

Screen Artist
Jill Proll

Illustrators
Ronda David-Burroughs
Cheryl Grubbs

About the Author

Lonzell Watson is an Apple Certified Professional with 15 years of experience as a professional photographer and videographer for news, wildlife, adventure racing, sports and special events. His work also includes writing, directing, and producing national commercials and television programs for PBS, Fox Sports, the Outdoor Channel, and C-SPAN, and video work for pop superstar Mariah Carey. He is the author of the *Canon VIXIA Digital Field Guide* and *Final Cut Pro 6 for Digital Video Editors Only,* both from Wiley Publishing and *Final Cut Express 4 Essential Training* from Lynda.com. Lonzell's talents have served him well as a syndicated writer with hundreds of published tutorials, and his syndicated content is read by thousands of industry professionals each month.

Author's Acknowledgments

Special thanks to Jody Lefevere, without whom this project would not have been possible, and thanks to project editor Jade Williams whose organizational precision and demand for excellence has made this book a truly creative and wonderful way to learn Apple iPhoto. I would also like to thank the graphics department for their outstanding work articulating complex concepts through amazing visual works of art. You guys are truly amazing. I would also like to thank technical editor Dennis Cohen for overseeing the accuracy of the exercises in this book as well as the terminology.

Special thanks go to Laura Clor, my lovely wife Robyn, Shannon Johnson, Lisa Waters, Danya and Sean Platt, Kimmi and James Patterson, for their assistance as I wrote this book.

Table of Contents

chapter 1 Getting Started with iPhoto

chapter 2 Bringing Photos into iPhoto

chapter 3 Organizing Your Photos

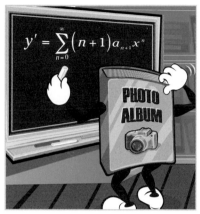

 **chapter 4** **Logging and Searching for Photos**

Table of Contents

chapter 7 Enhancing Your Photos

chapter 8 Showcasing Your Photos

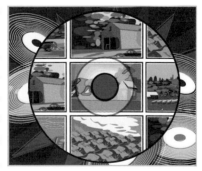

Table of Contents

chapter 11 Creating Photo Books

chapter 12 Creating Photo Calendars and Cards

Table of Contents

chapter 13

Memory Cards and Storage

CHAPTER 1

Getting Started with iPhoto

Apple designed iPhoto to help photographers manage and edit large numbers of digital images in a very easy and intuitive workflow. No matter the task, the iPhoto interface is designed so that the most important element of your work remains the main focus: the photographs. The iPhoto workflow is streamlined so that photographers of all skill levels can import, organize, edit, and share their photographic works of art.

Understanding iPhoto

Apple iPhoto is a powerful digital photo management and editing application. You can use iPhoto to import photos from your camera's memory card onto your computer for viewing, then organize and sort libraries of digital images in a variety of ways. iPhoto also possesses photographic darkroom tools that enable you to enhance colors, adjust tone, crop, and much more without altering the original image. iPhoto also enables you to distribute your photos by creating Web galleries and slideshows, and also by designing beautiful photo books, calendars, and greeting cards.

iPhoto Is Powerful and Easy to Use

Apple designed iPhoto so that photographers could apply most of their efforts to taking great photographs and less time tweaking them on a computer. By using a simple workflow of import, organize, edit, and share, iPhoto makes it easy for anyone to use its robust capabilities to design and distribute beautiful digital images.

iPhoto Is a Database

iPhoto enables you to organize a large collection of digital images along with their information, so that you can easily locate and sort photos. iPhoto retains the EXIF data the camera attaches to photographs, but also enables you to add additional information to the database as you rate and enhance images.

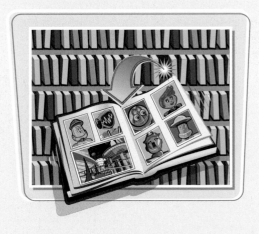

iPhoto Is an Organizational Tool

iPhoto enables you to group images by events, albums, and folders. You can view one image at a time or groups of images, while adding keywords and titles, and flagging and rating photos for increased organization. The viewing options enable you to view images as slideshows, side-by-side comparisons, or full screen.

iPhoto Is a Digital Photo Editing Tool

iPhoto also gives you control over the look of your images by enabling you to crop, straighten, rotate, adjust exposure and color, add special effects, and more. iPhoto also enables you to remove common photographic problems such as red-eye or use the retouch tool to remove minor blemishes. All changes to an image's appearance are nondestructive, which means iPhoto never saves a new version over the previous one, but regards all changes as an edit list that can be reverted back to the original image.

iPhoto Is for Presenting Your Photos

You can use iPhoto to set up print options for books, calendars, contact sheets, and greeting cards. iPhoto has a variety of options that enable you to quickly view photos as slideshows or screen savers, or showcase them in an online Web gallery. iPhoto also enables you to distribute your photos by burning them to CDs or DVDs.

Check Out the Features in iPhoto

Apple iPhoto is equipped with a wide array of features to help you locate, edit, and print your digital images. Once you have accumulated a large library of images, iPhoto enables you to efficiently locate specific images no matter where they are stored. You can also improve photos in iPhoto and quickly apply those adjustments to other photos, use Apple iPhoto themes, and print frame-worthy works of art with your desired look and feel.

Manage a Large iPhoto Library

iPhoto helps you locate a specific photo out of thousands of images through filters that use date, keyword, or rating. You can organize your photos based on who is in the image with facial recognition. iPhoto also uses data from the iPhone camera and GPS-enabled cameras to categorize photos by location. If you do not have an iPhone or GPS-enabled camera, you can add the location information yourself.

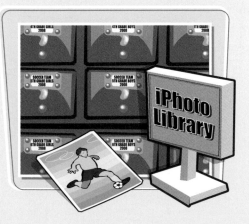

View Images as Themed Slideshows

iPhoto makes it simple for you to quickly play back your images as a slideshow using themes such as Scrapbook, Snapshots, and Ken Burns effect. Facial recognition is used during playback of the slideshow, so that no face appears off-screen.

Share Photos Online

You can quickly post your photos on Facebook and Flickr to share with friends and family without leaving iPhoto. When new photos are added to your Facebook account, iPhoto sends your friends notifications. When sharing images on Flickr, the location information that you assign your photos in iPhoto appears on Flickr photo maps. You can also share photos online using MobileMe, Web pages, and e-mail.

Enhance Photos

Perfect your photos by making a few simple adjustments using the iPhoto editing tools. iPhoto enables you to adjust saturation in your photos by using a slider, without affecting skin tones. The **Retouch** button ( ) in iPhoto removes spots and blemishes without blurring details. iPhoto also uses facial recognition to remove red-eye with a single mouse click.

Create Travel Maps

iPhoto uses the location information of your photos to create a custom map featuring all of the cities you visited. You can use these maps to create professionally printed photo books that feature vacation photos. Create a custom map by typing the locations you have visited and use them with any Apple book theme.

Streamline the iPhoto Workflow

iPhoto was designed to streamline the digital photographic workflow by enabling you to import the digital images from a camera, organize the photographs, edit them, and then share the images. Understanding the iPhoto workflow before you begin to import your photos gives you a clear blueprint on how to get the most out of the application.

Import Digital Photos

You begin to work with iPhoto by importing images from an electronic device or digital medium, or just an image file located on your Mac. You can import from a digital camera, CD, DVD, flash drive, or memory card reader. Scanned photos can also be used in iPhoto. To import your photos from an electronic device you must first make the necessary hardware connections.

Organize Your Photos

After you have imported a large number of images into iPhoto, sorting and categorizing photos makes them more easily accessible for manipulation. Imported photos are automatically organized by date into events and are placed in the iPhoto Library. You give the events specific names such as Family Reunion, Graduation, Birthday Party, and so on. To further organize the images, iPhoto enables you to rename, merge, and split events, as well as create photo albums and folders.

Edit Your Photos

iPhoto provides a number of tools that can help you fine-tune and enhance your photos. Use the iPhoto edit tools to crop, rotate, fix red-eye, adjust color and exposure, as well as add special effects. Edit photos to improve not-so-perfect photos and add a unique look and feel.

Share Your Photos

Now it is time to share your photos with others either in print or online. iPhoto has many options that enable you to create and order your own calendars, photo books, greeting cards, or to print your photos. Distribute your photos electronically by publishing photos to Facebook, Flickr, or MobileMe, designing your own blog, or creating photo CDs and DVDs.

Start iPhoto for the First Time

You can start iPhoto on your Mac and begin to import, organize, edit, and share your digital photographs.

Start iPhoto for the First Time

1 Click the **Finder** icon ( ) in the Dock.

You can also click the iPhoto program icon in the Dock to start the program and skip the rest of these steps.

The Finder window appears.

2 Click **Applications**.

3 Double-click **iPhoto**.

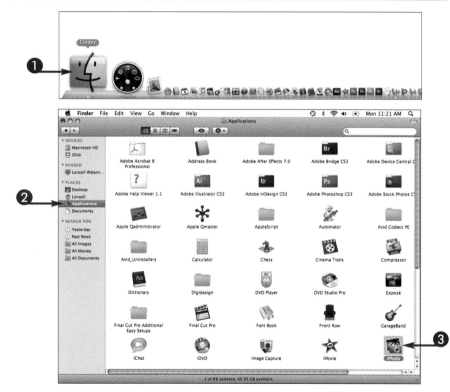

The Welcome to iPhoto '09 screen appears.

④ Click **Close**.

Note: *If there was an earlier version of iPhoto located on your computer, iPhoto asks to convert its photo library.*

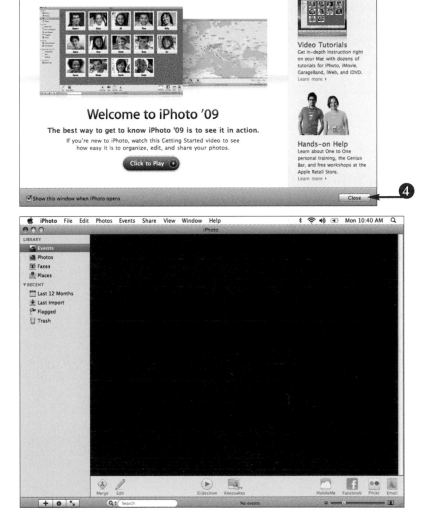

iPhoto starts.

Note: *To learn how to begin the process of importing photos from a digital camera, see Chapter 2.*

TIP

How can I prevent the iPhoto Welcome screen from launching each time I start iPhoto?

You can uncheck the **Show this window when iPhoto opens** option (☑ changes to ☐) at the bottom of the Welcome screen.

Explore the iPhoto Preferences

Although you can use iPhoto without changing any preferences, you can customize some of the ways iPhoto appears and functions. The iPhoto preferences enable you to customize your workspace to fit your needs so that you can work more efficiently. To access the Preferences window, in the main menu, click iPhoto and then click Preferences. You can now change the preferences according to your particular needs.

● **General**

You can select the General preference options to customize the basic functions of iPhoto, such as what happens when you double-click a photo and where photos are edited.

● **Appearance**

You can select the Appearance preference options to change the look of the iPhoto interface and how information is presented.

● **Events**

You can select the Events preference options to manage the function and organization of events.

● **Sharing**

You can select the Sharing preferences to enable photo sharing across a computer network, so that other iPhoto users can view your photos on their own computers.

General | Appearance | Events | Sharing | Web | Advanced

Sources: ☑ Show last 12 ⬍ months album
☐ Show item counts
Double-click photo: ○ Edits photo
● Magnifies photo
Rotate: ○ ↺ ● ↻
Edit photo: In main window ⬍
Email photos using: Mail ⬍
Connecting camera opens: No application ⬍

☑ Check for iPhoto updates automatically

● **Web**

You can select Web to configure and manage your MobileMe account as well as publish photos to your account.

● **Advanced**

You can select the Advanced preference options to manage photo importing, RAW image handling, and whether iPhoto looks up location information.

The iPhoto interface is designed so that your photos remain the center of focus throughout the entire iPhoto workflow, and so that you can concentrate on what matters most: the image. The General layout consists of four main parts that enable you to view, organize, edit, and search the iPhoto Library. Images can be reviewed and edited in full screen, where the interface switches to a neutral-grey-and-black color scheme, so that there is limited interference in color perception.

● **iPhoto Main Menu Bar**

The iPhoto main menu bar includes all of the main options for the open windows. The main menu bar gives you quick access to all of the iPhoto functions.

● **Source List**

The iPhoto Source list displays the organizational structure of all of the photos imported into iPhoto. From the iPhoto Source list you can access your photos based on their organization in the form of Events, Albums, Slideshows, and Projects.

● **Photo Viewing Area**

This area is for viewing and editing photographs. What appears here is largely dependent upon what is chosen in the Source list. If you are opening iPhoto for the first time, this area is empty because you have not imported any photos into iPhoto.

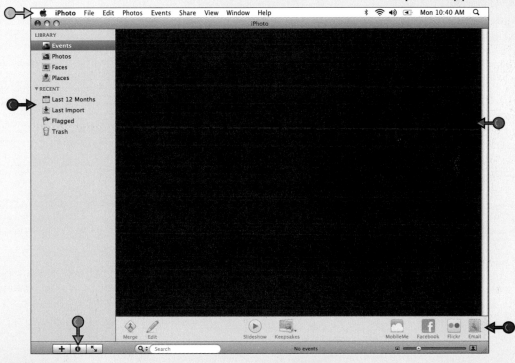

● **Information Pane**

The Information pane provides information on selected photos in the viewing area. If you have not selected a single photo in the viewing area, the Information pane displays information on the group of photos you have selected in the Source list.

● **Toolbar**

The iPhoto toolbar provides a number of buttons that enable you to search, edit, and share photos. The tools in the toolbar change, as does the availability of certain tools, depending on what is selected in the Source list.

Bringing Photos into iPhoto

Digital photography has opened the door for photographers to acquire images from a diverse lineup of electronic sources. iPhoto gives you the ability to import digital photos from a variety of sources, as well as providing unique ways to share your photographs with friends and family through RSS photo feeds. iPhoto can accommodate image files in many different file formats and provides you the convenience of accessing third-party applications to edit your photographs.

Understanding the iPhoto Import Process

The first step in organizing, editing, and sharing high-quality digital photographs with iPhoto is the import process. iPhoto enables you to import photos from various digital media and electronic devices, the most popular being a digital camera. iPhoto cannot import digital photographs unless it understands their file format. Fortunately, iPhoto supports photos that have been saved in a wide range of file formats such as JPEG, TIFF, RAW, PSD, and more.

Import Devices and Media

You can import images from electronic devices such as digital cameras, mobile phones, CDs, DVDs, flash drives and memory card readers into iPhoto. You can even import movie clips from digital still cameras with video capability. Scanned photos and other digital photo files can be imported into iPhoto from the desktop. To import photos from electronic devices, you must first make the necessary hardware connections from the device to the computer, typically with a USB cable.

Saving Time

If you are launching iPhoto for the first time, iPhoto asks if you always want it to run each time you connect a camera. Choose Yes to save yourself time. iPhoto asks this question because an application already on your Mac, named Image Capture, can download images. If you have already chosen not to have iPhoto launch when you connect a camera, you can open the iPhoto preferences, click the General tab, and then choose iPhoto from the Connecting camera opens option.

Do you want iPhoto to run each time you connect your camera? Yes ⦿ No ○

01:17

Import Photos that Are Not Digital

If you have shoeboxes of old photographs lying around, you can use a scanner to scan the photographs into digital files and import those files into iPhoto. If your camera used 35mm film, you can take your negatives to a company that specializes in digital imaging services and have them transfer the images to a CD or place them on the Web. After the photos are in digital form, you can import them like any other photo stored on your computer hard drive.

Location of Imported Files

Upon import, iPhoto makes copies of the image files and immediately categorizes them into events, which are stored in the iPhoto Library located in the Pictures folder on your computer hard drive. The path to the iPhoto Library from your desktop is: Macintosh HD > Users > User's Name (This is probably your name) > Pictures > iPhoto Library. The original image files remain untouched, unless you tell iPhoto to erase the camera's memory card after importing. After import, you can give each event a descriptive name and even combine (merge) events.

Backup iPhoto Library

Now that you know where the iPhoto Library can be found on your computer, you should consider backing up your photos. It is quite possible that iPhoto will house your entire collection of photos, so an occasional backup would prove very important to the preservation of your photographic work. You can use the Burn command in Finder to burn backups to CDs or DVDs.

After the Import

When you have imported all of your files into iPhoto, the next thing you want to do is review them. There is a level of excitement upon seeing your photographs for the first time, possibly in full screen; this is a good time to weed out any images that you do not deem worthy of keeping. Any bit of housekeeping that you do at this point helps with the organizational process in iPhoto.

Understanding File Formats

The character code extension that follows the name of the file lets the Mac Operating System look in Launch Services to see whether an association has been made for that file extension, or file type. iPhoto supports photos that have been saved in a wide range of file formats such as JPEG, TIFF, RAW, PSD, and more.

JPEG

You will sometimes see this file format listed as JPEG or JPG. JPEG is the most common file format digital cameras use. A digital camera creates a JPEG file by processing and compressing the data received from the image sensor. The compression which occurs in the creation of a JPEG file can create undesired digital artifacts in photographic images.

TIFF

You will sometimes see this file format listed as TIFF or TIF. TIFFs are very large, high-quality image files that may or may not be compressed. Some cameras utilize a compression algorithm for lossless storage and enable you to save your images as TIFF files. TIFFs are great for image editing and can possess multiple layers and support an alpha channel.

RAW

RAW files are unprocessed image files and are a true representation of the data gathered by the camera's image sensor. Because RAW files retain so much of their image data, you can perform dramatic edits, such as huge shifts in exposure, without losing quality. RAW files take up much more space on memory cards than do JPEG files.

PSD

PSD is the standard file format produced by Adobe Photoshop and Photoshop Elements. PSD files can also contain multiple layers.

GIF

GIF is the most commonly used file format for non-photographic elements. Many of the logos and banners that you encounter online are GIF files.

PNG

The PNG format is also popular for Web graphics and was actually created to possibly replace the GIF format. PNG24 supports transparency and is also a lossless alternative to JPG.

PDF

The Portable Document Format was created for document exchange. You will find many help menus, online user's manuals, and Read Me files provided in this format.

SGI and TGA

The SGI and TARGA (TGA) file formats are used for high-end Silicon Graphics workstations and Truevision video-editing systems.

FPX

Chances are, you may not have heard of the FlashPix file format with the extension .fpx. This file format is also used in Web design.

PNTG

Apple Computer released the PNTG file format with MacPaint, its first graphics-painting program, which shipped with the original Macintosh personal computer in 1984.

Connect a Digital Camera, Card Reader, and the iPhone to Your Computer

You can import photos from a variety of digital devices into iPhoto to begin to organize, edit, and share your photographs. Digital cameras, card readers, and the iPhone use a simple USB connection to the USB port in the computer.

Connect a Digital Camera, Card Reader, and the iPhone to Your Computer

Note: Some cameras, including video cameras that also take still pictures, need to be placed in the correct mode before you can import.

① Plug the 4-pin connector into the USB porton the Mac.

Note: You can also plug it into a USB hub.

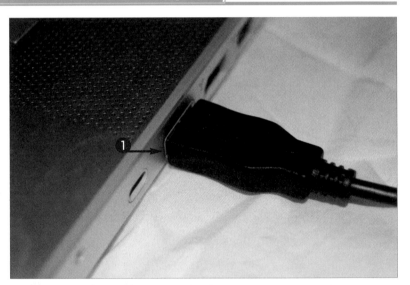

② Plug the other end of the USB cable into the device.

Note: The iPhone uses a Dock connector to the USB cable. Plug the wider Dock end into the phone. The connection should be very obvious.

③ Turn on the device, if it is not already turned on.

Note: Make sure you insert the memory card into the card reader, if you are connecting a card reader.

iPhoto launches and you can see the photographic contents of the device.

④ Click **Import All**.

What can I do if iPhoto does not see the camera when I connect it to the computer?

If iPhoto does not see the device after you have made the connection, try turning the device off and then on again. If this does not work and iPhoto continues to not see the camera, you can take the memory card out of the camera and place it into a card reader, and then connect the card reader to the computer.

Import from a Digital Camera, Card Reader, and the iPhone

You can import photos from a digital camera, card reader, and the iPhone and save them on your computer. If iPhoto has been configured to launch when a camera is connected to the computer, it launches upon making the connection and turning on the device.

Import from a Digital Camera, Card Reader, and the iPhone

① Connect your digital device to your Mac.

The iPhoto application launches and the device appears in the iPhoto Devices section.

② Type a new name in the **Event Name** text box for the group of photos you are about to import.

③ Type a description of the group of photos you are about to import.

④ Click **Hide photos already imported** (☐ changes to ☑).

iPhoto hides the photos that have been previously imported so that you do not try to import them again.

Note: *You can uncheck **Autosplit events after importing** (☑ changes to ☐) if you do not want iPhoto to split photos into separate events according to date.*

⑤ Press the ⌘ key and then click to select each photo you want to import.

⑥ Click **Import Selected** to import the selected photos.

Note: *If you want to import all photos on the device, click **Import All**.*

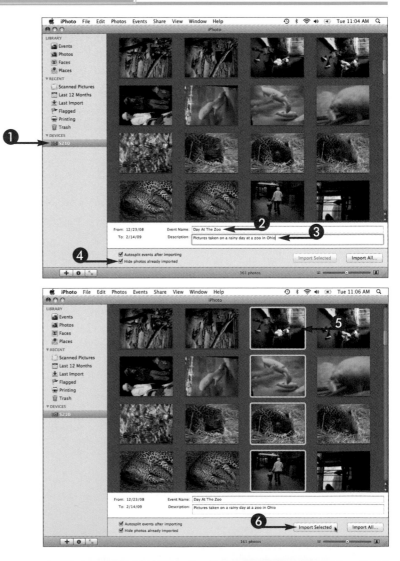

iPhoto imports the photos from the device.

7 If you want iPhoto to delete the photos on the memory card or digital device after import, click **Delete Photos**.

*Note: Click **Keep Photos** if you want to keep the photos on the memory card or device.*

8 Click **Last Import** to view the new photos.

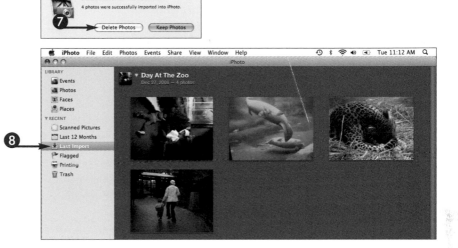

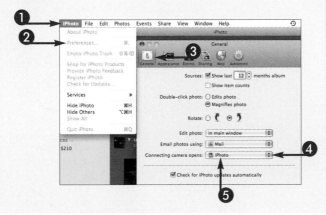

TIPS

How can I set iPhoto to open, instead of Image Capture, after I connect my digital device?

Follow these steps:

1 Click **iPhoto** in the main menu.

2 Click **Preferences**.

3 Click **General**.

4 Click the Connecting camera opens ⬍.

5 Choose **iPhoto**.

Can I import video into iPhoto from my digital still camera that is video capable?

Yes, only if the digital still camera uses QuickTime-supported video formats. Upon import, the first frame of the video file is shown in the iPhoto Library along with a camera icon and the file's duration. You must double-click the video thumbnail to play it. The video file will play in the QuickTime player.

Import from Your Hard Drive, CDs, DVDs, and Flash Drives

You can choose to navigate to locations on your computer hard drive and import photos into iPhoto. iPhoto gives you the convenience of importing individual or multiple files, including folders of photographs.

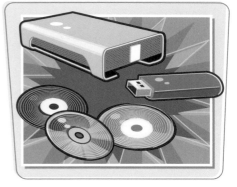

Import from Your Hard Drive, CDs, DVDs, and Flash Drives

Note: *To import from a flash drive, you will need to have it inserted in the computer port before beginning the following instructions.*

① Click **File** in the main menu.

② Click **Import to Library**.

The Import Photos dialog opens.

③ Navigate to the location of the photos you want to import.

You can navigate to a specific hard drive, mounted disc icon, or thumb drive to import photos.

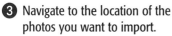

4 Select one or more photos to import.

Note: You can also choose folders for import.

5 Click **Import**.

The imported photos appear as an untitled event under Last Import within the Source list.

Can I drag and drop photos into iPhoto?
Yes. The quickest way to import photos from the desktop into iPhoto is to drag and drop. You can drag and drop single or multiple images, including folders, into the iPhoto main viewing area to import. You can also drag directly onto an album in the Source list, a folder, or an existing Event to add photos.

How do I get my shoebox full of old photographs into iPhoto?
You can place your old photographs into a scanner and create a digital file that can be imported by following the steps in this task. If you have a 35mm camera, you can go to a professional digital-imaging company and have them make you a CD of your photos.

Import Photos from Web Pages

You can easily save graphics from friends' Web sites into the iPhoto Library while using the Safari Web browser.

① Click the Safari icon () in the Dock.

The Safari window opens.

② Navigate to the Web page that has the graphic you want.

③ Right-click, or **Control**-click the graphic you want.

A contextual menu opens.

4 Choose **Add Image to iPhoto Library** from the menu.

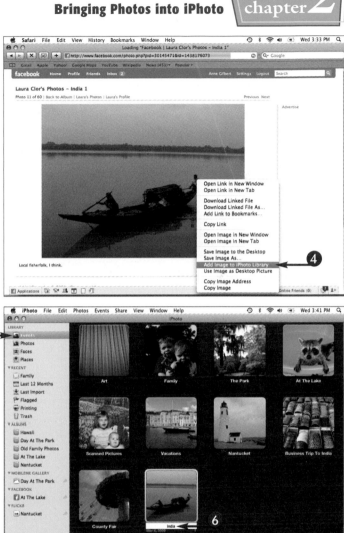

iPhoto opens if it is not already open.

The photo is imported into the iPhoto Library.

5 Click **Events**.

6 Name the new event for the imported image.

Note: You can also merge the event with a preexisting event.

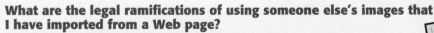

TIP

What are the legal ramifications of using someone else's images that I have imported from a Web page?

Be mindful of images that you save from the Internet for commercial use because they may be subject to copyright. For more information on copyright law, visit www.copyright.gov.

Move Photos from iPhoto to Photoshop

You can import photos and take advantage of some of the quick-fix edit features such as the Enhance tool, Red-Eye, and Rotate. For more-complex editing, you can choose to open iPhoto photographs into a more sophisticated image-editing program such as Adobe Photoshop.

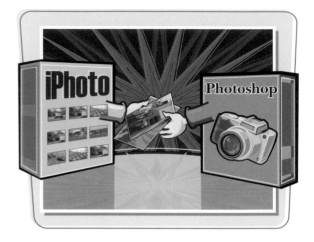

Move Photos from iPhoto to Photoshop

① Click **iPhoto** in the main menu.

② Click **Preferences**.

The iPhoto preferences open.

③ Click **General**.

④ Click the **Edit photo** ▼.

⑤ Choose **In application** from the pull-down menu.

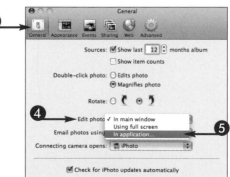

The application folder opens.

6 Click the Adobe Photoshop folder.

7 Click the Adobe Photoshop application icon.

8 Click **Open**.

Adobe Photoshop appears in the Edit photo pull-down menu.

9 Click to close the iPhoto preferences.

When you select a photo, click Edit () in iPhoto, the photo opens in Adobe Photoshop.

Note: *You can also right-click (*Control*-click) a photo in iPhoto and choose to edit in full screen within iPhoto, or edit in an external editor. This will allow you to use iPhoto as the default editor, and edit in Photoshop when needed.*

Note: *When you are finished editing the image in Photoshop, save the image in its current file format, and the changes will be reflected in iPhoto.*

Is this the easiest way to open my iPhoto photos in Photoshop?

No, there is a quicker and easier way. You can simply drag a photo thumbnail from iPhoto and drop it on top of the Adobe Photoshop program icon in the Dock. You can also drag multiple images at a time this way to edit them in Photoshop.

Are there any drawbacks to dragging and dropping photos from iPhoto to Adobe Photoshop?

Yes. iPhoto does not have the ability to make a backup copy of the image if you drag and drop it onto another program icon, so you lose the benefit of being able to revert back to the original state of the file.

CHAPTER 3

Organizing Your Photos

One of the main purposes of iPhoto is to streamline the process of managing large numbers of imported photos. All images that you import into iPhoto are stored in the Library, which resides in the Source list. Upon import, photos can be automatically organized into a structured filing system called Events. You can then sort your photos into subcategories such as personalized Albums or folders, which can be named after a vacation, reunion, or birthday party. iPhoto also enables you to further customize photo organization by setting preferences.

Explore the iPhoto Source List

All of your imported photos are organized and can be accessed in the iPhoto Library located in the Source list. Connected devices such as the iPod and iPhone also appear in the Source list. The Source list is home to the projects you create inside of iPhoto such as slideshows, Web galleries, and Keepsakes such as photo books, calendars, and cards. iPhoto makes it easy for you to locate and access any group of photos from the Source list. The contents of each category in the Source list appear in the photo-viewing area to the right.

● **Library**

All of the photos transferred from external sources are stored in the iPhoto Library. Upon import, every photo is automatically grouped according to the time it was taken; each group is referred to as an Event. All photos in the library are stored under the Photos icon. The Library also provides unique ways of browsing and searching for people and places by using the Faces and Places icons.

● **Events**

When photos are imported into iPhoto they are automatically grouped into Events. A thumbnail of a photo contained within the group, called a *key photo*, represents each Event. By default, the first photo in the Event is the key photo, but you can designate a different photo. You can position your cursor over each Event icon to skim through the thumbnails of each photo represented in that group. You can merge, split, rename, and move photos between Events.

● **Photos**

Click the Photos icon (▣) to reveal individual thumbnails of all photos in the Library. This can be a massive list of photos depending on how large your photo collection has grown.

● **Faces**

Faces gives you a quick way to identify and browse photos that contain specific friends and loved ones using iPhoto's facial recognition. You can use Faces to begin photo projects such as books, calendars, and cards.

● **Places**

Use Places to browse and search photos taken in a specific location while using a camera with GPS capability. You can manually apply location data to photos taken with a camera that is not GPS capable. Places enables you to create professional travel maps that you can include in your photo projects such as books, calendars, and cards.

● **Recent**

The Recent options give you the ability to quickly return to what you were working with last, which can come in handy as your iPhoto Library grows. The first option under Recent uses the name of the Event you last opened in the Events category.

● **Devices**

Any external device such as a digital camera, iPod, or iPhone connected to the computer appears in the Source list under the Devices category, along with an icon of the device. Some devices display an Eject icon to unmount the device; for others you will have to `Control`-click and choose Unmount from the menu options.

● **Albums**

Albums are subsets of pictures located in the iPhoto Library. Use Albums to organize your photos further than just by time or date. You can create categories such as: Hawaii, Day At The Park, and Old Family Photos. Groups of related Albums can be placed into folders for increased photo management.

● **MobileMe Gallery, Facebook Gallery, and Flickr Gallery**

Any of the Web galleries that you create using MobileMe, Facebook, or Flickr appear in the Source list. You can view the contents of the Web site by clicking a gallery icon, or, you can add to the gallery by dragging and dropping a photo onto it.

● **Keepsakes**

The photo books, calendars, and cards that you create are kept under Keepsakes. Click one of the project icons to edit the photo project.

● **Slideshows**

Saved slideshows are found under the Slideshows category. You can click any of the saved slideshows appearing in this category and further edit the slideshow or delete it.

Modify Autosplit into Events

The Autosplit into Events option in iPhoto preferences enables you to dictate how imported photos are organized as Events. You can configure iPhoto to organize groups of photos by days, weeks, or even two- or eight-hour time periods. The Autosplit into Events option provides you increased photo management flexibility upon import.

① Click **iPhoto** in the main menu.

② Click **Preferences**.

The Preferences dialog opens.

③ Click **Events**.

④ Click the **Autosplit into Events** ⬍ and choose **One event per week** from the pop-up menu.

Upon import, iPhoto imports photos from a week-long vacation as one Event.

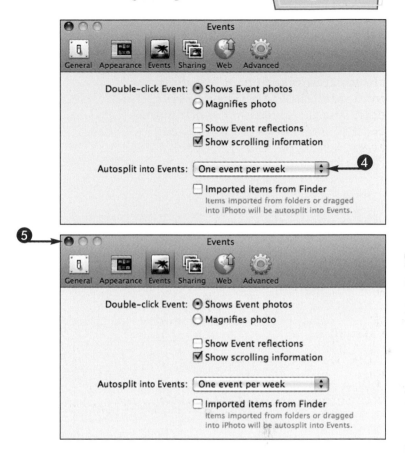

⑤ Click 🔘 to close the window.

iPhoto now autosplits into Events at the specified frequency.

TIP

Can iPhoto autosplit a group of photos taken on different days upon import?

Yes. If you took pictures at a birthday party on Wednesday, then at the lake on Friday, and took more pictures at a wedding on Saturday, iPhoto can split the photos into three Events upon import. Check **Autosplit events after importing** at the bottom of the import window.

☑ Autosplit events after importing
☐ Hide photos already imported

Split Events

iPhoto can autosplit Events after they have already been created. If you choose an autosplit option that includes photos from different dates in the same Event, iPhoto can conveniently separate the Events.

① Click **Events** in the Source list.

② Choose the Event that you want to split.

③ Click **Events**.

④ Click **Autosplit Selected Events**.

The photos are split into separate Events by date.

5 Click **untitled event** under the new Events.

6 Type a new name for the Event(s).

7 Repeat Steps **5** and **6** for any remaining untitled Events.

Can I split an Event other than by date?

Yes, you can open an Event and choose the photo where you want the split to occur. Click **Events** in the main menu bar and then click **Split Event**. Every photo after the photo you selected is split from the preceding photos. The selected photo becomes the first photo in the new Event.

Events	Share	View	Window	Help

Create Event
Create Event From Flagged Photos
Split Event
Make Key Photo
Add Flagged Photos To Selected Event
Open in Separate Window

Autosplit Selected Events

Merge Events

You can merge two or more Events with photos taken on various dates and combine them into a single Event. Merging Events helps you to manage a very large collection of photos.

① Click **Events** in the Source list.

② Select the Events that you want to merge.

Note: *You can* ⌘ *-click multiple Events or drag a selection around multiple Events.*

Yellow selection boxes appear around the chosen Events.

③ Click the **Merge** button (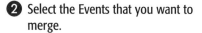).

Note: *You can click* **Events** *and choose* **Merge Events**.

A dialog appears asking if you want to merge these Events.

④ Click **Merge**.

The Events merge into one Event named after the first Event chosen during selection.

Is there a quicker way to merge Events?

Yes. Click and drag an Event and drop it on top of another Event. A dialog appears asking if you want to merge these Events. Choose **Merge**. The Events merge into one Event and it is named after the last Event onto which the photos were dropped.

Can I change the thumbnail that represents the Event?

Yes. Roll the mouse cursor over the thumbnail to skim through the Event and stop on the image that you want. Press Spacebar on the keyboard and the new image becomes the key photo.

Create a Custom Event

You can create a custom Event from selected photos in the iPhoto Library. The ability to create custom Events enables you to pick and choose which specific photos are contained in an Event. Custom Events provide you more photo management control.

1 Click **Photos** in the Source list.

2 Select the photos that you want to include in the custom Event.

Note: You can drag a selection around multiple photos or ⌘-click multiple photos to select nonadjacent photos.

A yellow selection box appears around the chosen photos.

3 Click **Events**.

4 Click **Create Event**.

The Create New Event dialog opens.

5 Click **Create**.

● The photos are placed into the Event and now you can name the new Event and change its date.

Can I create an empty Event to move photos into it at a later time?
Yes, you can create an empty Event that you can later populate with photographs. This is a great option if you are currently unsure which photos will go into the new Event. Make sure no photos are selected in iPhoto. Follow these steps:

1 Click **Events** in the Source list.

2 Click **Events**.

3 Click **Create Event**.

The new empty Event appears.

Move Photos Between Events

You can easily move photos between Events by dragging them from one Event and dropping them into another. The ability to move photos between Events provides you another option for creating custom Events that contain specific photos of your choosing. Keep in mind that although a photo can belong to only one Event, it can also be in many Albums. It may prove more convenient to employ Albums as a means of organizing photos for use in slideshows, books, and other projects.

Move Photos Between Events

① Click **Events** in the Source list.

② ⌘-click the two Events you want to move photos between.

Note: *You can also drag a selection around multiple adjacent Events.*

③ Double-click one of the selected Events.

Both Events open and are separated by a dividing line in the middle.

④ Click and drag the photos you want to move and drop them into the other Event.

The photo has now been moved to the other Event.

⑤ Click **All Events** to return to the previous view.

The previous screen appears displaying all Events.

What can I do with photos that I do not want to move or delete?
iPhoto enables you to hide photos that you do not want to move or delete. Control-click the photo you want to hide and choose **Hide Photo** from the menu.

| My Rating ▶ |
| Make Key Photo |
| Hide Photo ◀ |
| Move to Trash |
| Revert to Original |

How do I bring back hidden photos?
When you view photos in an Event that contains hidden photos, iPhoto makes you aware that there are hidden photos by providing the message Show hidden photos. Click the **Show hidden photos** message in the upper-right corner of the Event. The hidden photo appears with an orange X. Control-click the photo and choose **Unhide**.

Show 1 hidden photo ← →

Name Photos Using Faces

iPhoto can locate and group the people in your photo library using facial detection and recognition. You can assign names to faces of friends and family members and iPhoto will recognize them when you import new photos. Faces makes it easy for you to find photos of specific people instead of manually searching through groups of photos.

Note: *When you first open iPhoto, you may notice next to the Faces icon in the Source list that iPhoto is scanning the photos in your library that contain faces. Let the scan complete before you begin these steps.*

① Pick a photo that has a face of the person you want to name.

② Click the **Name** button (▣).

The photo enlarges and a positioning box appears over the face or faces in the photo.

Note: *You can drag the corners to make the box smaller or larger.*

③ Click the **unknown face** text at the bottom of the positioning box.

④ Type the name of the person whose face is in the positioning box.

Note: You can now click the arrow button to move to the next picture. If iPhoto thinks that it recognizes a previous person you have named, iPhoto suggests a name.

Note: If iPhoto suggests the correct name, a check mark appears in the name field that you can click to accept the name, or, click the X to reject it.

⑤ Click **Done** once you have finished naming faces.

⑥ Click **Faces** in the Source list to reveal the named Faces.

iPhoto displays a snapshot on a corkboard of all of the people you have named.

Note: An information icon appears as you position the mouse pointer ( ) over the bottom right corner of the snapshot. You can click the information button to flip the snapshot and add information such as full name and e-mail address.

TIPS

What do I do if I have multiple faces in my photograph?

If you have more than one face that you need to name in a photo, click the **Name** button and position the mouse pointer over the other faces to reveal the positioning box and then add their names.

Why does the positioning box not appear in my photo after I click Name?

It is possible that iPhoto has not scanned the photo or did not recognize there was a face in the photograph. Click the **Add Missing Face** button to make the positioning box appear and continue with Steps **3** to **9** in this exercise.

Add Missing Face

Confirm Names with Faces

iPhoto enables you to find more photos
containing the faces you have just named. You
can double-click one of the snapshots to reveal
more pictures that iPhoto believes contain the
named face. Once you confirm the faces in other
photos, iPhoto makes it easy to build photo
slideshows, books, calendars, and cards of your
friends and family.

① Click **Faces** in the Source list.

The named faces appear as
snapshots on a corkboard.

② Double-click one of the snapshots.

The photo that you named
appears at the top of the viewing
area. iPhoto places the
photographs that it believes
contain the person at the bottom
of the viewing area.

③ Click the **Confirm Name** button
(image).

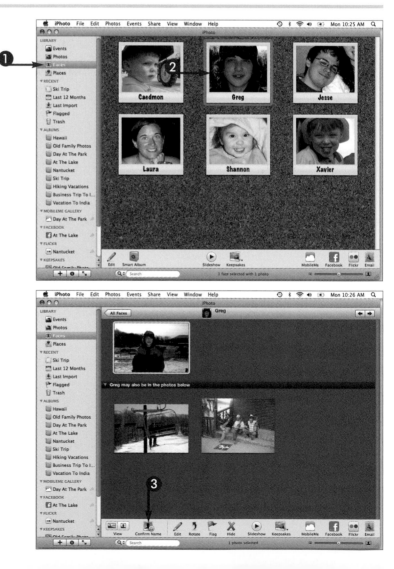

The photo that iPhoto needs you to confirm has the text "click to confirm" at the bottom.

④ Click once on a photo to confirm the name or twice to reject it.

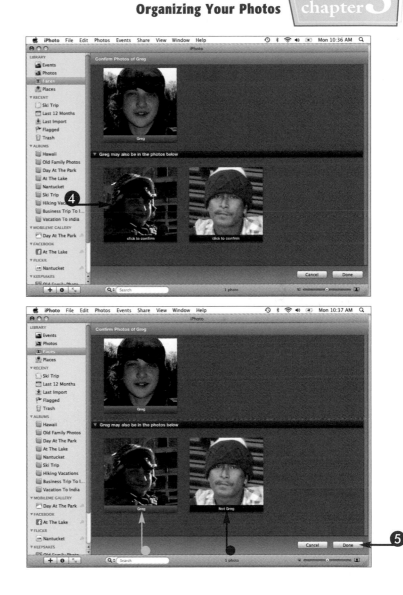

● When you click once on a photo to confirm, the bottom of the photo turns green.

● When you click twice on a photo to reject it, the bottom of the photo turns red.

⑤ Click **Done** when you are finished confirming names.

How does Faces help me to make projects of my friends and family?

After you have confirmed names, your snapshots under Faces act like an Album or Event. To create a project that consists of a particular person, you only have to select the snapshot and choose the project.

Add Locations Using Places

When you import a photo from a GPS-enabled camera into iPhoto, iPhoto imports the location data and maps it automatically. If your camera does not have GPS capability, you can manually add a location to your photos. Places enables you to conveniently browse and organize photos based on the location in which they were taken.

Note: iPhoto requires an internet connection to view the Places maps.

① Select the photo to which you want to add the location.

Note: You can perform these steps on an entire Event.

② Click the **Information** button (ⓘ).

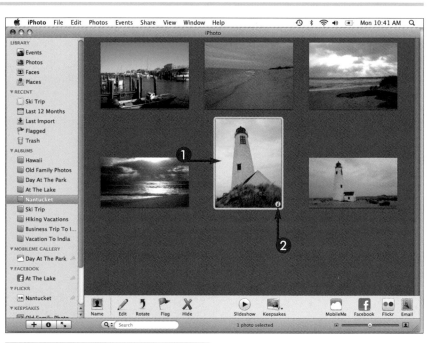

The photo thumbnail flips around so that you can enter the location information on the back.

Note: The photo will already have location information with pinpoints and a map if the camera with which it was taken had GPS capability.

③ Click the **Enter photo location** field and type the information.

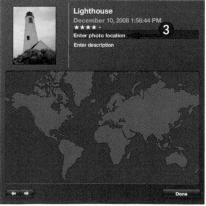

As you begin typing, a list of possible locations appears.

④ Choose a location from the list.

● You can now see the location pinpointed on the map.

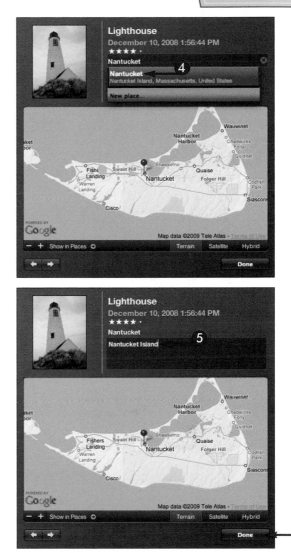

⑤ Click in the **Enter description** field and type a description.

⑥ Click **Done**.

iPhoto turns to the previous screen.

 TIP

What if the location I am looking for is not on the list?

You can choose New place at the bottom of the menu and use Google Search to pinpoint the location. Follow these steps:

① Type the location into the field.

② Click **New place** at the bottom of the menu.

The Edit My Places window opens where you can utilize Google Search to pinpoint the location.

Explore Photos Using Places

Once you have assigned locations to your photos you can click Places in the Source list to browse your photos by location. The Places view provides you a map complete with pinpoints marking the locations of all your photos. The Map view provides a unique way to browse your photos.

Note: *iPhoto requires an internet connection to view the Places maps.*

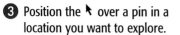

① Click **Places** (🔲) in the Source list to enter Map view.

A map appears with pins designating the locations of your photos.

② Double-click the map to zoom into it.

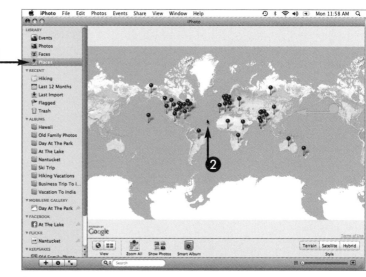

③ Position the ↖ over a pin in a location you want to explore.

The location name appears.

④ Click the arrow to the side of the location.

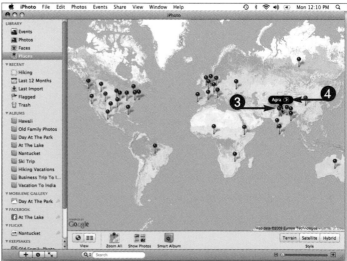

The photos appear that have been taken in that area.

⑤ Click **Map** to return back to Map view.

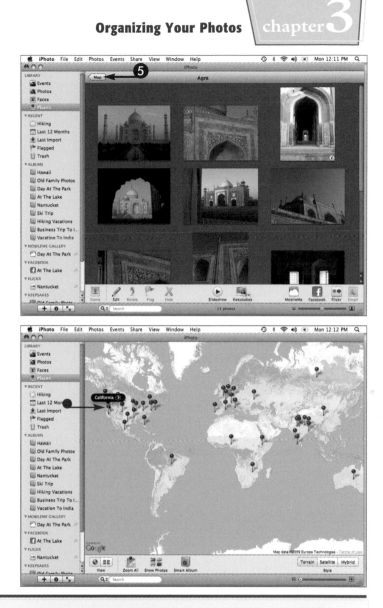

● You can explore another location by positioning your ▶ over a pin.

TIPS

Can I view the photos taken from an entire region?

Yes. You can zoom into a specific region and click **Show Photos** (). The photos taken in that entire region are shown.

Are there any other views by which I can browse photos by location?

Yes. You can browse your locations as a list. Click the right side of the **View** button () to view places as a list. Click a location in the columns to view the photos taken at those locations. For a more pointed search, you can click locations in the first, second, third, and fourth columns.

Create a Photo Album

You can create an Album to store a collection of photos with a similar theme. Photos in an Album are just pointers to the original photographs. Creating an Album in the iPhoto Library enables you to include only the photos that you want to view.

CREATE A NEW ALBUM

① Click **File** in the main menu.

② Click **New Album**.

Note: You can also press ⌘ + N on the keyboard to create a new Album.

③ Type a name for the new Album.

④ Click **Create**.

The new Album appears in the Source list.

ADD PHOTOS TO AN ALBUM

1 Click **Photos** in the Source list.

2 Select the photos that you want to add to the new Album.

3 Click and drag the photos to the new Album in the Source list.

4 Repeat Steps **2** and **3** to add other photos to the new Album.

5 Click the new Album.

iPhoto displays the photos you added to the Album.

Note: *You can drag and drop or copy and paste photos between Albums.*

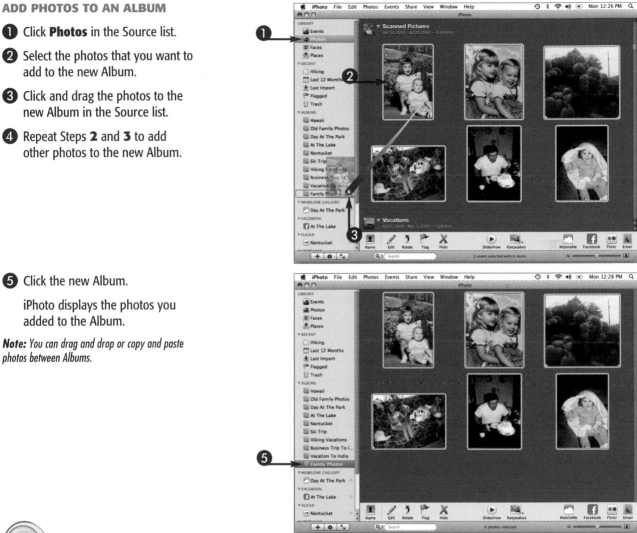

Is there a faster way to add photos to an Album?

Yes. When you click **Photos** in the Source list, you can select a group of photos that you want to add to the new Album. You can then click **File** in the main menu bar and click **New Album From Selection**. Type the new Album name and then click **Create**.

Create a Smart Album

You can automatically create Smart Albums from photos that meet common criteria, such as Description, Date, Filename, or any text for which you want to search. Smart Albums can save you the effort of sorting through photos in the iPhoto Library.

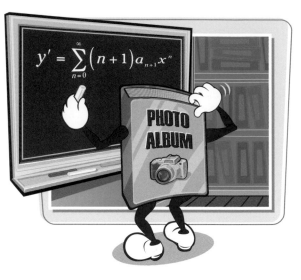

1 Make sure no photos are selected and click the **Add** button (⊞) in the bottom left corner of the iPhoto interface.

*Note: You could also click **File** in the main menu then choose **Smart Album**.*

2 Click **Smart Album**.

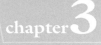

③ Type a name for the Smart Album.

④ Click ↕ and choose the criteria used to populate the Smart Album from the pop-up menu.

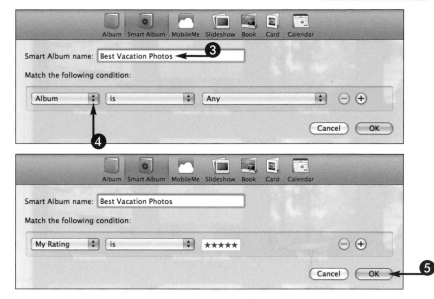

⑤ Click **OK**.

iPhoto creates the smart Album and populates it with photos that possess the specified criterion.

Note: *Additional criteria can be added by clicking the Plus button (⊕) at the bottom right.*

 TIPS

Is there a faster way to create a Smart Album?

Yes. To create a Smart Album from a Faces group, click the **Faces** icon in the Source list, then drag a group of photos to an empty part of the Source list. A Smart Album with the same name as the Faces group is created.

Can I edit the criteria of my already created Smart Album?

Yes. You can edit the criteria for a Smart Album that appears in the Source list to add photos. Click the Smart Album in the Source list and then click **File** and then click **Edit Smart Album** to specify new criteria.

Merge Albums

iPhoto enables you to combine the photos contained within multiple Albums for more organization. You can merge Albums that contain similar content such as a vacation in India and a business trip to India so all of the India photos can be found in one Album.

① Click **File** in the main menu bar.

② Click **New Album**.

③ Give the new Album a name appropriate for the multiple photos you will merge.

④ Click **Create**.

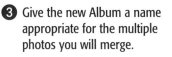

The new Album appears in the Source list.

5 Select the Album in the Source list whose contents you want to merge.

● The contents of each Album appear in the photo viewing area.

6 Press ⌘ + A to select all of the thumbnails in the photo viewing area.

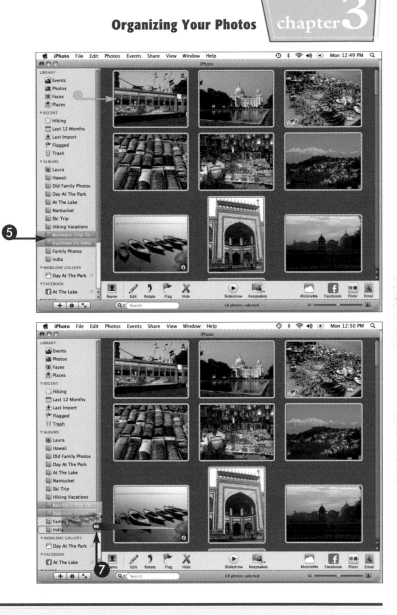

7 Drag the selected thumbnails to the new Album in the Source list.

The contents of the Albums are copied into the new Album.

TIP

Are there other ways to organize Albums?

Yes. As your photo collection grows, so does your list of Albums in the Source list. You can use folders to organize your Albums and salvage some real estate in the Source list. Click **File** in the main menu and choose **New Folder**. You can then drag the actual Albums in the Source list into the new folder.

File	Edit	Photos	Events	Share
New Album...				⌘N
New Album From Selection...				⇧⌘N
New Smart Album...				⌥⌘N
New Folder				⌥⇧⌘N
Smart Album Info				⌘I
Import to Library...				⇧⌘I
Show Aperture Library...				
Export...				⇧⌘E
Close Window				⌘W

Back Up the iPhoto Library with Time Machine

Time Machine provides an efficient way to back up your computer, including the iPhoto Library. Periodically backing up your iPhoto Library helps to protect your photo collection from accidental erasure and file corruption. Time Machine requires a second volume and you must set up Time Machine before you begin backing up your files.

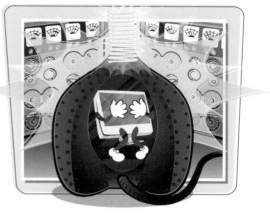

Back Up the iPhoto Library with Time Machine

Note: Have an external drive already connected to your computer and turned on before beginning these steps.

① Click **Apple** (🍎) in the main menu.

② Click **System Preferences**.

System Preferences opens.

③ Click **Time Machine** (🕐).

The Time Machine pane appears.

④ Slide the switch from **OFF** to **ON** if Time Machine is OFF.

A list of drives opens.

⑤ Pick the drive on which backups will be stored.

Note: *The hard disk you choose may have to be reformatted. Reformatting your hard disk erases everything on the drive! Consider using an empty drive for storing backups.*

⑥ Click **Use for Backup**.

Time Machine performs an initial backup of the entire system.

Note: *After Time Machine has backed up your computer, you can search through your backups within iPhoto by clicking File in the iPhoto main menu and choosing Browse Backups.*

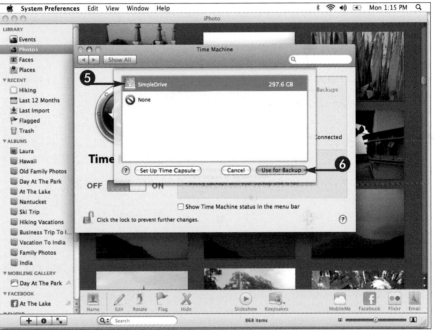

Are there any other ways to back up my photo library?

Yes. If you are a MobileMe member you can use the Backup utility to copy your iPhoto Library to your iDisk. You can also burn backup files to CDs and DVDs. The iPhoto Library is located in the Picture folder on your computer.

Can I initiate a backup?

Yes, you can initiate a Time Machine backup. Click and hold down the mouse on the Time Machine icon in the Dock, then choose **Back Up Now** from the menu.

Create a New iPhoto Library

You can create multiple iPhoto Libraries to store your Albums, slideshows, books, calendars, and cards. Creating multiple iPhoto Libraries is a good option for managing a very large collection of photos. Dividing your large photo collection into separate libraries also improves the performance of iPhoto, especially when scrolling.

Create a New iPhoto Library

① Click **iPhoto** in the main menu.

② Click **Quit iPhoto** to close the application.

③ Press and hold Option while you click the **iPhoto** Dock icon to launch iPhoto.

④ Click **Create New**.

A dialog opens.

5 Type a name for the new library.

6 Click the **Where** ⬦ and choose a location for the new library from the pop-up menu.

Note: You can click the Expand button (▼) to navigate the entire computer system and create a new folder wherever you want.

7 Click **Save**.

iPhoto opens and the empty iPhoto Library appears in the Source list.

Note: All newly imported photos are stored in the new library.

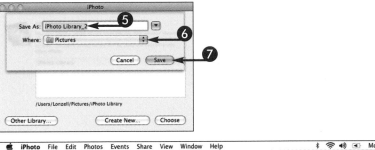

How do I move between libraries?

You can move between multiple iPhoto Libraries by quitting iPhoto, then pressing and holding **Option** while you click the **iPhoto** Dock icon to launch the application.

When the dialog opens you can click the **Choose** button to specify which iPhoto Library to access.

Are there other options for navigating between libraries?

Yes. There is a shareware program called iPhoto Library Manager that provides more flexibility for moving between iPhoto Libraries. Check out iPhoto Library Manager at www. fatcatsoftware.com/iplm/?.

CHAPTER 4

Logging and Searching for Photos

"Florida Sunset"

Keywords - Florida, sunset, honeymoon, beach, getaway, landscape, July, Katie, Jim, newlyweds

An important aspect of how iPhoto makes it easier to manage large numbers of imported photos is through its logging and searching capabilities. Properly logging photos with descriptive names, providing ratings, flagging images, and adding keywords enables you to more efficiently search an iPhoto Library that contains many photographs. iPhoto offers a number of searching mechanisms to quickly find your photos, including searching by date, keyword, rating, location, or even by person.

Using Photo Information

The information that you provide for imported photos, including titles, descriptions, and keywords, makes the task of searching for photos in the iPhoto Library easier. Knowing the type of photo information at your disposal enables you to use the iPhoto searching mechanisms more effectively.

Titles and Descriptions

The title and description that you give a photo or group of photos after import play a significant role in your ability to later locate that photo. The original file name on the hard drive can also be used to locate an image using the Search box at the bottom of the iPhoto viewing area.

Flagging Photos

You can flag photos to temporarily group or identify them for later use, such as for editing or using in a book, calendar, or card. You can flag photos to sort out a particular group of images from the larger collection and create a new Event or simply delete them.

Using Keywords

Keywords are searchable descriptive words that you can use to find photos in the iPhoto Library. Think of keywords as labels that you can use to find photos of a specific category such as Family, Favorite, and Vacation. You can also edit keywords to rename them or assign keyboard shortcuts by forming a quick-pick list.

"Florida Sunset"
Keywords - Florida, sunset, honeymoon, beach, getaway, landscape, August, 2009, Katie, Jim, newlyweds

Rating Photos

You can assign a 1 to 5 star rating to photos to indicate their quality or how much you like them. You can use ratings to automatically create albums and sort through the iPhoto Library. Ratings provide a great way to gather all of your highest-quality photos to use in a project.

Image and Camera Information (Metadata)

You can view iPhoto's stored Exchangeable Image File (EXIF) information, which includes the image size, date, the time the image was taken, camera type, and GPS latitude and longitude. GPS capability is usually limited to a few higher-end Digital SLR camera models and is rare among point-and-shoot cameras. The Places functionality of iPhoto uses this information to determine the location in which the photo was taken with a GPS-enabled camera.

title **Butterflies in a Field**
date **7/28/09**
time **2:45:52 PM**
rating • • • • •
keyword **butterfly**
kind **JPEG Image**
size **2048 x 1536**

Access and Edit Photo Information

iPhoto stores information such as title, description, date, time, rating, and keywords for each of the photos in the library. The Information pane provides a quick way to view the photo information. The Information pane also provides you a way to edit photo information.

ACCESS PHOTO INFORMATION

1 Click the photo for which you want to view its information.

Note: You can also view the information for a group of photos including name, description, and the amount of hard drive space it uses.

2 Click the **Information** button (🛈).

● The Information pane opens.

Note: To access camera specifications and GPS data, select a photo and click Photos and then click Show Extended Photo Info from the main menu.

EDIT PHOTO INFORMATION

1 Click in the Title field and type a new title.

Note: You can type in any of the fields in the Information pane to edit the information.

2 Click the **Information** button ⓘ again to close the Information pane.

The Information pane closes.

TIP

Is there another way to edit photo information?

Yes. You can edit photo information directly underneath the photo. If you do not see the information under the photo, click **View** and then choose **Titles**, **Rating**, or **Keywords**. You can then click in the information field under the picture and type the new data. As a second alternative, you can roll the mouse pointer over the bottom right corner of the photo and click the **Information** icon. The photo flips over and you can specify a name, supply a rating, add a location, and enter a description.

Edit Photo Information for a Group of Photos

You can edit the information for a group of photos all at once in iPhoto. Making batch changes to photo information saves you a lot of time as opposed to manually editing each photo's information one by one.

Edit Photo Information for a Group of Photos

1 Click a group of photos in the Source list that contains the photos for which you want to change information.

2 ⌘-click or drag a selection around the photos for which you want to edit the information.

3 Click **Photos** in the main menu bar.

4 Click **Batch Change**.

Note: You could also press Shift + ⌘ + B on the keyboard to access the Batch Change options.

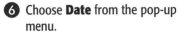
A dialog appears, letting you change photo information.

5 Click the **Set** 🔽.

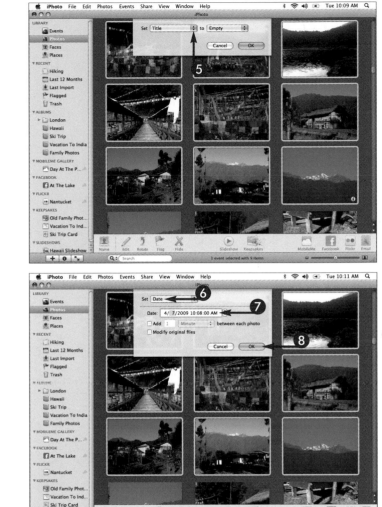

6 Choose **Date** from the pop-up menu.

7 Click the date and time field and type new values.

Note: *You can also use the arrow keys to change the values of the highlighted areas in the date and time field.*

8 Click **OK** when finished.

The new date and time are applied to the group of photos.

TIPS

Why would I change the date and time for my photos?

iPhoto uses the date and time information to organize your photos. The clock in your camera could be broken and you need to add the correct dates. If you have a group of old photos that you have scanned, you may want the date to reflect the actual date they were taken and not the date on which they were scanned.

Does iPhoto change the original date and time in the file when I edit the information?

If you click the Modify original files option, iPhoto changes the original date and time in the file. If not, it only notes the change in the iPhoto database.

Set [Date] to

Date: 4/ 7/2009 10:12:39 AM

☐ Add 1 Minute between each photo
☑ Modify original files

Cancel   OK

Flag Photos

You can flag photos for editing or use in a future project such as a slideshow, photo book, calendar, or card. Flagging enables you to quickly identify a group of images within the iPhoto Library for a given task.

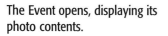

① Click **Events** in the Source list.

iPhoto shows all events.

Note: *You can flag photos from any group.*

② Double-click an Event thumbnail that contains photos that you want to flag.

The Event opens, displaying its photo contents.

③ Select the photos that you want to flag.

Note: *You can press* ⌘ *+* A *to select the entire contents of the Event.*

④ Click the **Flag** button (🚩).

- A flagged indicator appears in the top-left corner of the photographs.

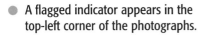 Click **Flagged** in the Source list to view all flagged photographs.

The flagged photos are revealed in the main viewing area.

How do I create a new Event with flagged photos?

You can drag flagged photos from their current group and drop them into a new Event, or you can go to Events and then choose **Create Event From Flagged Photos**. You can also select an empty Event and go to Events and choose **Add Flagged Photo To Selected Event**.

How do I unflag a photo?

As soon as you flag a photo or group of photos, the Flag button turns into the Unflag button. If you do not want a photo to remain flagged you can select the photo and then click the **Unflag** button ( ).

Assign Keywords

You can assign keywords to those photographs that fall under a common category such as Family, Vacation, and Birthday. iPhoto has several predefined keywords by which you can categorize your photographs, or you can create your own custom keywords. Because keywords are searchable, they can be used to categorize photos and make locating images easier.

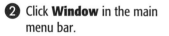

① Click a group of photos in the Source list to which you want to assign keywords.

② Click **Window** in the main menu bar.

③ Click **Show Keywords**.

Note: *You can also press* ⌘ *+* K *on the keyboard.*

The Keywords options appear.

④ Select one or more photos for which you want to assign a keyword.

⑤ Click the keyword in the Keywords dialog that you want to associate with the selected photos.

The keywords are assigned to the photo.

Note: You can assign multiple keywords to photos.

Note: You can remove the keyword by clicking the keyword again in the Keywords dialog.

⑥ Click to close the Keywords dialog.

Is there another way to add keywords?

Yes, you can type a keyword directly underneath the photos by clicking **View** in the main menu bar and choosing **Keywords**.

How do I make my own keywords?

You can make your own keywords by clicking the **Edit Keywords** button in Step **5**. In the Edit Keywords dialog, select an existing keyword and then click **Rename** to type a new keyword, or press the **Create a New Keyword** button (⊞) to create a new one.

Using Keyboard Shortcuts for Keyword Favorites

You can easily assign keywords to photos by creating one-character keyboard shortcuts. After you have designated your favorite keywords and created a keyboard shortcut, you can select photos, and then press the shortcut on the keyboard to assign it. Assigning keyword shortcuts can save you time.

Using Keyboard Shortcuts for Keyword Favorites

① Click a group of photos in the Source list for which you want to assign keywords.

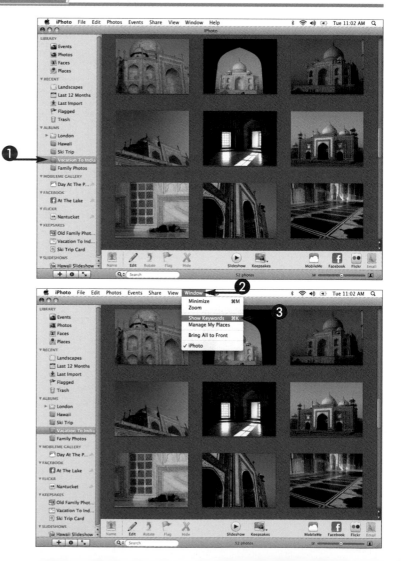

② Click **Window** in the main menu bar.

③ Click **Show Keywords**.

Note: You can also press ⌘ + K on the keyboard.

The Keywords options appear.

④ Click and drag **Favorite** from the bottom half of the Keywords dialog and drop it into the upper half of the dialog.

● The keyword appears in the upper part of the dialog along with the assigned one-character keyboard shortcut inside of it.

Note: iPhoto uses the first letter of the keyword to create a keyboard shortcut. If that letter is already being used for another shortcut, it uses the second letter in the specified keyword.

⑤ Select all of the photos in the photo group for which you want to assign the keyword "Favorite."

⑥ Press **F** on the keyboard to assign the keyword to the specified photos.

How do I change the keyboard shortcut iPhoto created?

You can change the keyboard shortcut that iPhoto automatically created by clicking **Edit Keywords** pictured in the Keyboards options in Step **4** and then following these steps:

① Click in the **Shortcut** field of the preferred keyword.

② Type a new keyboard shortcut.

③ Click **OK**.

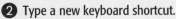

iPhoto uses a five-star system to enable you to rate the photographs in your collection. Rating photos can help you quickly sort the great photos from the not-so-great photos.

① Click a group in the Source list containing photos that you want to rate.

② Select the photo or photos that you want to rate.

Note: *You can* ⌘ *-click to select nonadjacent photos.*

③ Click **Photos** in the main menu bar.

④ Click **My Rating**.

⑤ Choose the number of stars to award the photograph.

The rating is assigned to the individual photo or group of photos.

6 Click **View**.

7 Click **Rating**.

You can now view the rating under the photo thumbnails.

Is there a faster way to rate photos?

You can supply a rating to photographs faster using a keyboard shortcut than navigating through the main menu bar. You can select a photo or multiple photos and press ⌘ along with a number key from 1 to 5 to rate a photo.

How do I remove a rating?

You can remove a rating by clicking **Photos**, choosing **My Rating**, and then selecting **None** from the menu. You can also remove a rating pressing ⌘+0.

Locate Photos by Text

You can search for photos using text that can be found in the photo information such as the title and description. You can even perform a search for the original file name of a photo on the hard drive. Photo information can help you quickly sort through a large photo collection when you are looking for something specific.

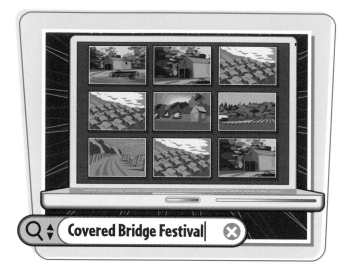

Locate Photos by Text

① Click **Events** in the Source list.

All of the Event thumbnails appear in the viewing area.

Note: Clicking the Events icon in the Source list enables you to search the entire iPhoto Library for folders. You can also select the specific Event, album, or folder where you know the image resides.

② Click the **Search** icon (🔍) in the Search box.

The Search pop-up menu appears.

③ Click **All** from the menu to search for text.

Note: You can also search by Date, Keyword, and Rating.

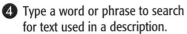

④ Type a word or phrase to search for text used in a description.

The photos with the specific text that you type appear in the viewing area as you type.

Note: You can also type a location or names of people to perform a search.

⑤ Click the **Reset** button (⊗) in the Search field to clear the search after you have finished.

All photos appear again in the viewing area.

TIPS

Why did my search results come up empty when I know the image is in the library?

If your search result comes up empty, you may have a specific album selected which does not contain the photo. If you have a particular album selected as you perform a search, iPhoto looks inside only that album for the text you enter.

What do I do if I am missing a photo?

You can click the trash can icon in the Mac's Dock to see if it is in there. You can search all files and folders on your computer by clicking the Spotlight icon (🔍) at the far right of the main menu bar and enter the text you are searching for in the box that appears. You could also import the photograph again.

Look for Photos by Date

You can search for photos by date using a calendar. The calendar offers a Year view consisting of 12 buttons, one for each month, and also a Month view that features 28 to 31 dates depending upon the month. Searching for photos by date makes it easy to search for photos when you do not remember their names.

① Click **Events** in the Source list.

All of the Event thumbnails appear in the viewing area.

Note: *Clicking the Events icon in the Source list enables you to search the entire iPhoto Library for folders. You can also select the specific Event, album, or folder where you know the image resides.*

② Click 🔍 in the Search box.

The Search pop-up menu appears.

③ Click **Date** from the menu.

The calendar opens, showing the individual months in the year.

④ Click a month to display the photos taken in that month.

The photos taken within that specific month and year appear in the viewing area.

Note: *Months for which no photos were found are grayed out. You can also position the mouse pointer over particular months to reveal how many photos are in that month.*

⑤ Double-click a month to reveal dates in the month.

The days of the month appear.

⑥ Click a date to reveal photos taken on that date.

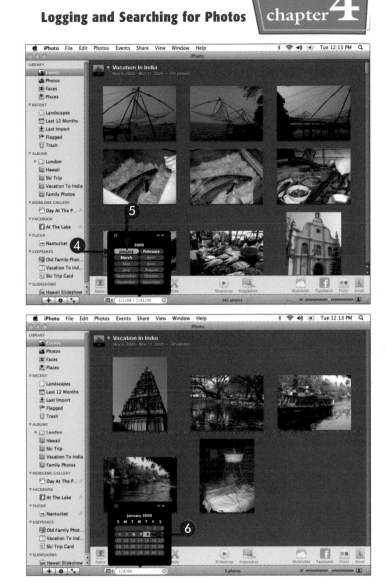

Can I display photos for multiple months at a time?

Yes. You can display multiple months at a time by pressing Shift on the keyboard and clicking another month. The search field displays the time frame from which the search was taken. You can also press and hold Option and click the arrows in the upper-right corner of the calendar to choose the same month for multiple years.

Search for Photos by Keyword

You can search for photos by keywords you have previously assigned. Searching for photos by keyword makes it easy to find specific photos in a large photo collection.

① Click **Events** in the Source list.

All of the Event thumbnails appear in the viewing area.

Note: *Clicking the Events icon in the Source list enables you to search the entire iPhoto Library for folders. You can also select the specific Event, album, or folder where you know the image resides.*

② Click 🔍 in the Search box.

The Search pop-up menu appears.

③ Click **Keyword** from the menu.

The list of keywords opens.

Note: *You can position the mouse pointer over a keyword to reveal how many photos have that particular keyword assigned.*

④ Click a keyword to find photos assigned that specific keyword.

The photos that were assigned that particular keyword appear in the viewing area.

Note: *You can also click the check mark to view photos that you have assigned check marks.*

⑤ Click the **Reset** button () to cancel the search.

All photos appear again in the viewing area.

TIPS

Can I narrow my search by using multiple keywords?

Yes. You can assign multiple keywords to a photograph, then click multiple keywords in the Keywords list to narrow a search.

Can I exclude certain keywords from a search for photos that have multiple keywords?

Yes. If you perform a keyword search for Family, but want to exclude a picture that also contains a coworker, you can Option-click Coworker.

Locate Photos by Rating

You can search for photos by ratings that you have previously assigned. Searching for photos by rating enables you to display only your favorite photos to use in projects or your least favorite photos so that you can dispose of them.

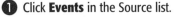

① Click **Events** in the Source list.

All of the Event thumbnails appear in the viewing area.

Note: *Clicking the Events icon in the Source list enables you to search the entire iPhoto Library for folders. You can also select the specific Event, album, or folder where you know the image resides.*

② Click 🔍 in the Search box.

The Search pop-up menu appears.

③ Click **Rating** from the menu.

A row of five dots appears.

④ Click the fifth dot to specify that five stars is the minimum amount of stars a photo must have.

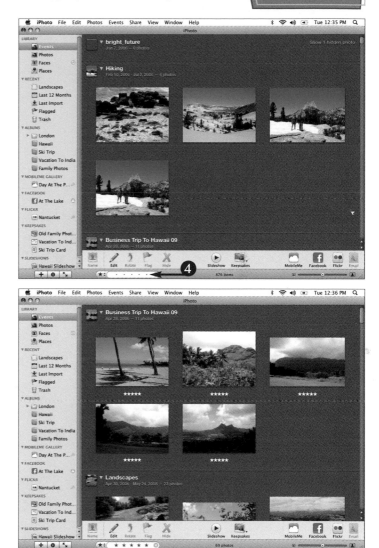

Only the five-star photos appear.

Note: If you choose a rating of four or fewer stars, photos with higher ratings also appear in the viewing area.

How can I display only photos with a specific rating such as three stars?

In order to get photos with the exact rating you have searched for to appear, you need to create a new Smart Album. Go to **File** in the main menu and choose **New Smart Album** and specify the rating for photos to be included in the album.

Sort Events

iPhoto displays the Events in the library in chronological order based upon the earliest date for any photo in the Event. You can rearrange how Events and photos are displayed by sorting them.

Sort Events By Title

Sort Events

① Click **Events** in the Source list.

② Click **View** in the main menu bar.

③ Click **Sort Events**.

④ Click **By Title**.

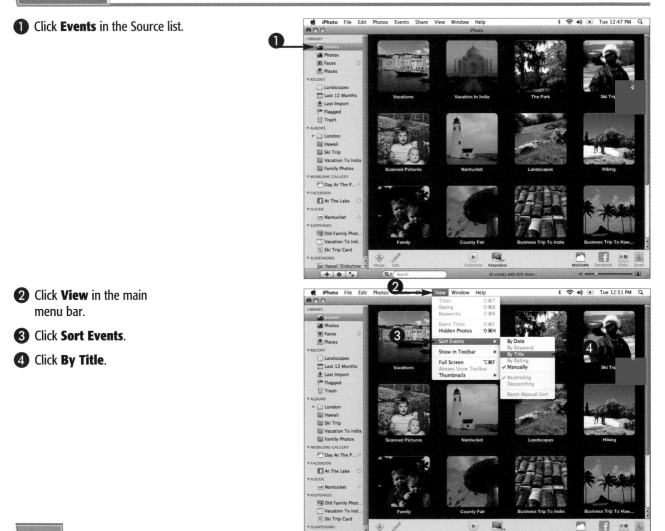

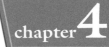 chapter 4

The menu closes and the Events are sorted in alphabetical order in the viewing area.

5 Click **View** in the main menu bar.

6 Click **Sort Events**.

7 Click **Descending**.

The Events are listed in reverse alphabetical order.

How do I view my most recently imported Events?

You can view the most recently imported Events in iPhoto by clicking the **Last Import** icon (🖼️) located in the Source list. Your most recent imports appear in the iPhoto main viewing area complete with the name of the Event, dates, and the number of photos imported.

CHAPTER 5

Viewing Photos

The iPhoto interface is designed so that the photographs remain the main focus of interest as you organize, edit, and share them. The iPhoto Source list acts as a giant digital shoebox of which photos are then shown in the photo viewing area. iPhoto enables you to view your photos in a variety of different ways to accommodate the task at hand. The viewing options include the ability to do photo comparisons, viewing at full screen, and zooming in and out of photos for a closer look.

Change the Event View

The Events pane in iPhoto Preferences enables you to view event photos in a variety of ways. You can choose what happens when you double-click an event thumbnail. By default, when you double-click an event, thumbnails of all of the photos within the event are shown in Photo view. You can set the preferences so that a single photo is magnified when you double-click an event thumbnail.

Change the Event View

1 Click **iPhoto** in the main menu bar.

2 Click **Preferences**.

The iPhoto Preferences dialog opens.

3 Click **Events**.

4 Click the **Magnifies photo** option (◯ changes to ◉).

5 Click the Close button (⬤) to close the Preferences dialog.

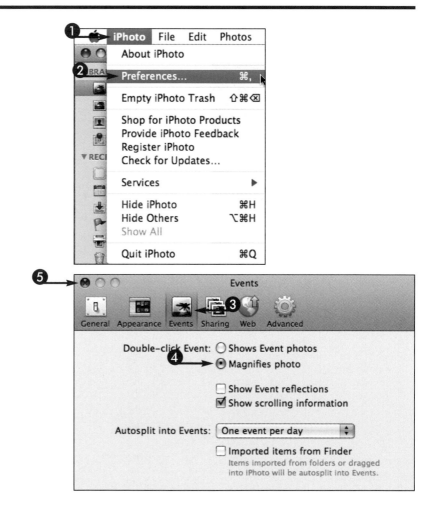

The Preferences dialog closes.

⑥ Click **Events** in the iPhoto Source list to display all events that have been created in iPhoto.

⑦ Roll the mouse pointer (🔺) back and forth over an event thumbnail to skim through all of the images contained in the event.

⑧ Double-click the photo that you want to magnify.

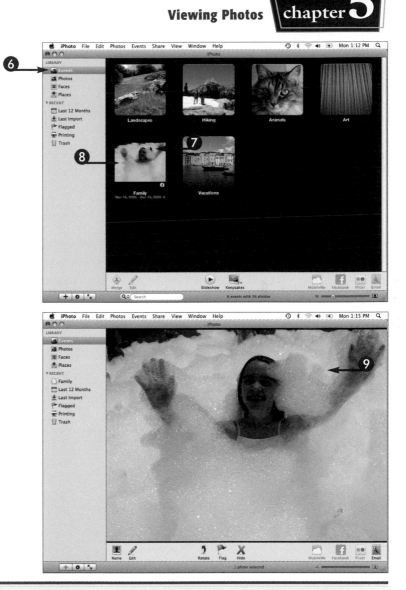

The photo is magnified.

Note: *You can view the entire contents of an event in a separate window by clicking once on the event thumbnail, then going to* **Event** *and clicking* **Open in Separate Window**. *This is a great way to focus on a specific event, and access other photos in the library.*

⑨ Click the magnified photo to shrink it and go back to the event thumbnail.

TIPS

Is it possible to see the entire contents of an event in the event thumbnail without skimming?

Yes. If you set the "Double-click Event" option to "Magnifies photo" in the preferences, all the contents of the event can be shown as a grid of photos. Place the mouse pointer (🔺) over the Show Photos button (Show Photos). You can also click Show Photos to open the event to reveal all of its pictures.

Can I change the size of the event thumbnails and the photos contained in them?

Yes. You can change the size of all photo thumbnails by using the size slider (⊙) located in the lower-right corner of the iPhoto interface. Drag the size slider to the right to increase the size of photo thumbnails.

View and Navigate Photos at Full-Screen

You can use iPhoto's full-screen view to view photos and to navigate backward and forward through the photos in a folder.

① Click **Photos**.

② Click the photo you want to view.

③ Click the **Enter Full Screen** button (⬈).

iPhoto displays the photo in full-screen mode.

④ Move the ➤ to the bottom of the screen.

⑤ Click the **Move to the Next Photo in Full Screen Mode** arrow (➡) to view the next photo in the folder.

Note: Move the ➤ to the top of the screen to reveal the photo browser and jump between nonconsecutive photos.

⑥ Click the **Exit Full Screen** button (⊗).

Note: You can also press the Escape key on the keyboard to exit Full screen.

iPhoto exits full-screen mode and returns to the previous screen.

Perform Full-Screen Photo Comparisons

iPhoto enables you to do a side-by-side comparison of photos while in full-screen view or in edit view. You can also choose different photos to compare. The ability to perform side-by-side comparisons helps you maintain consistency when editing a group of photos.

Perform Full-Screen Photo Comparisons

① Click **Photos**.

② Click one of the photos that you want to compare.

③ ⌘-click the second photo that you want to compare.

A selection box surrounds each of the photos you have chosen.

Note: *You can compare more than two images at a time by* ⌘ *-clicking multiple photos.*

④ Click .

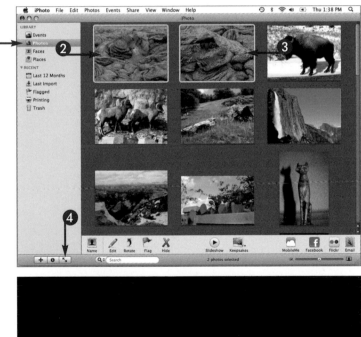

iPhoto displays both photos in full-screen view with a selection box around the second image.

⑤ Move the ↖ to the bottom of the screen.

⑥ Click .

iPhoto provides a comparison with the next image in the folder by switching the selected photo.

⑦ Click ⊗ when you are done.

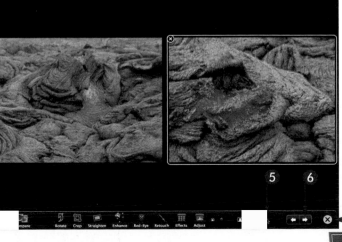

Zoom In and Out of Photos

iPhoto enables you to enlarge or reduce the size of photos while viewing them in edit view. Having the ability to zoom into photos gives you an opportunity to examine your photographs more closely for retouching images, red-eye reduction, and for cropping small areas of the image.

Zoom In and Out of Photos

ZOOM INTO THE CENTER OF PHOTOS

1 Click **Photos**.

2 Click the photo that you want to view.

3 Click the **Edit** button ().

The photo opens in edit view.

4 Drag the **size slider** (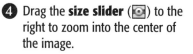) to the right to zoom into the center of the image.

● The Navigation window displays the magnified part of the image.

Note: You can drag the 🔘 all the way to the left to return the image to its original size.

ZOOM IN AND OUT OF SPECIFIC AREAS OF PHOTOS

1 Position the ⬉ over the area of the image that you want to zoom in to.

2 Press 1 on the keyboard to magnify the image by 100 percent or 2 for 200 percent.

The image is zoomed into around the area of interest.

Note: Press 0 on the keyboard to zoom out.

TIP

Can I zoom into the center of the image without using the mouse pointer?

Yes. Remove the mouse pointer (⬉) from over the top of the image, and then press 1 on the keyboard to magnify the photo by 100 percent or press 2 to magnify the image by 200 percent. You can press 0 on the keyboard to zoom out of the image.

Can I zoom into a photo that I have placed into a photo book template in iPhoto?

Yes. You can use the size slider located at the bottom-right corner of the iPhoto interface to zoom in and out of a page in a book, calendar, or card template.

Change the Look of Viewing Areas

You can set iPhoto to display a white, grey, or black background when viewing photos in Photo view. Changing the background color can help images light or dark in nature stand out from the background when searching through them.

① Click **Photos**.

② Click **iPhoto**.

③ Click **Preferences**.

The iPhoto Preferences open to reveal the last category that was viewed.

④ Click **Appearance**.

⑤ Click and drag the Background slider (⬤) from the default light shade of gray to black.

The background changes from shades of gray to black.

Note: You do not have to click and drag the slider to change the background color; you can click anywhere along the slider to adjust the color.

⑥ Click ⬤ to close the preferences.

Your viewing area reflects your changes.

When I scroll up or down while in Photos, an overlay appears indicating the date on which that particular batch of photos was taken. How do I hide this scrolling information?

Follow Steps **1** to **4** to access the iPhoto preferences. Uncheck **Show scrolling information** (☑ changes to ☐) to hide the scrolling information as you scroll.

July 2009

Add a Reflection Below Events

You can change the way events appear by adding a reflection of the event's key photo below the event. Changes in appearance can be made strictly for aesthetic reasons.

① Click **Events**.

② Click **iPhoto**.

③ Click **Preferences**.

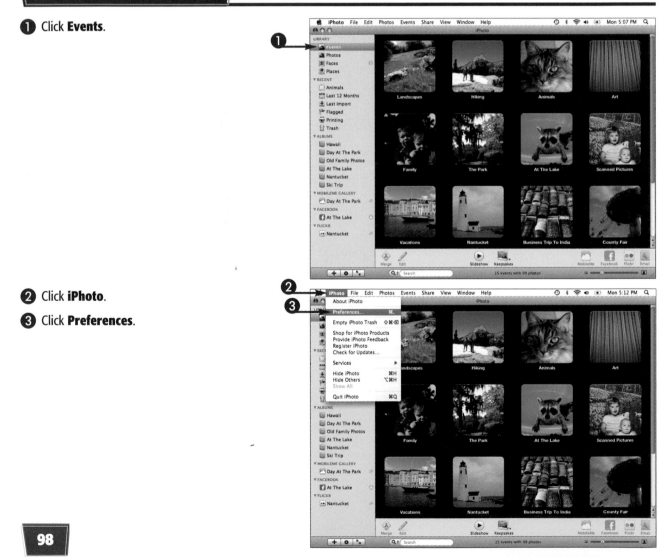

The iPhoto Preferences open to reveal the last category that was viewed.

④ Click **Events**.

⑤ Click the **Show Event reflections** option (☐ changes to ☑).

⑥ Click ◉ to close the iPhoto preferences.

A reflection now appears below each event's key photo.

Are changing background color and adding reflections to events the only things I can do to change the appearance of viewing areas?

No. You can also choose to add borders to photo thumbnails, add or remove drop shadows, and organize the view in the Appearance pane in the iPhoto preferences. You can also choose to change the font size from small to large. Depending on which view you are in, you can change the size of thumbnails as well as zoom in and out of photos, photo books, calendars, and card pages using the size slider.

Set a Photo as Your Desktop Wallpaper

You can set iPhoto to display a photo as computer desktop wallpaper. This is a great option for showcasing your photographs for friends, family, and co-workers.

Set a Photo as Your Desktop Wallpaper

1 Click **Photos**.

2 Click the photo that you want to use as wallpaper.

③ Click **Share**.

④ Click **Set Desktop**.

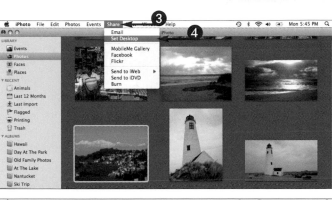

The photograph appears as your desktop wallpaper. If the dimensions of the photo is smaller than your computer screen, by default, the photograph is tiled to fill the space. If the photo is larger than the screen, it is centered and cropped.

Note: You can crop the image in iPhoto to the correct size ratio for your computer display. See how to crop images in Chapter 6.

How do I change my wallpaper photo?

You can change the photo that you designated for your wallpaper by following these steps:

① Click another photo you want to use as wallpaper in iPhoto.

② Click **Share**.

③ Click **Set Desktop**.

The new photograph appears as your desktop wallpaper.

Using a Group of Photos as Desktop Wallpaper

You can also have the desktop cycle through a series or group of images. This is a great way to showcase a series of images for friends, family, and co-workers.

Using a Group of Photos as Desktop Wallpaper

① Click a group of photos in the Library, from an Album, or one of the Recent photo options.

② Click **Share**.

③ Click **Set Desktop**.

The images begin to cycle on the desktop and the Desktop & Screen Saver System Preferences pane opens.

④ Click the **Desktop** tab.

⑤ Click 🔼 and choose how the photos will be scaled to fill the screen from the pop-up menu.

⑥ Click 🔼 and choose the screen duration for photos from the pop-up menu.

⑦ Click 🔘 to close the Desktop & Screen Saver preferences.

Your group of images cycles on the desktop according to the time duration you set in Step **6**.

Note: *You may have to crop the images to the proper size of your desktop in order for them to properly fit your computer screen. iPhoto can detect your screen resolution and place it as an option under Crop.*

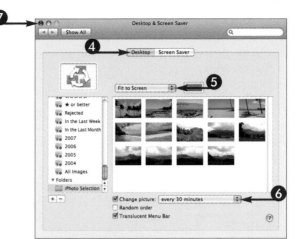

How do I change my wallpaper back to my original Mac OS X wallpaper?
If you want to change the wallpaper back to one of the Mac OS X wallpapers, you have to access the Mac OS X System Preferences and choose a wallpaper. Follow these steps:

① Click the **Apple** icon (🍎) in the Mac OS X.

② Click **System Preferences**.

③ Click **Desktop & Screen Saver** and choose an Apple Images category.

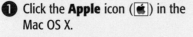

Basic Image Editing

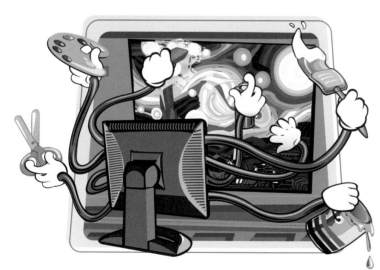

The photo processing tools in iPhoto are powerful, but easy to use. All edits performed on photographs are nondestructive, so you can safely retouch images, apply effects, crop, and straighten to improve photographs without altering the original image. iPhoto makes it easy for you to make all of your photographs the best they can be.

You can alter photos in iPhoto by selecting a photo and clicking the Edit button to enter the Edit view. The Edit view makes it easy for you to edit photos by giving you quick access to editing tools, and the ability to easily navigate groups of folders and change viewing options.

● Row of Thumbnails

At the top of the Edit view you will see a group of thumbnails that represent the adjacent photos within the same album, event, or library of the current photo being edited. Click another thumbnail to choose another image from the group to edit. In a large collection of photos, use the scroll bar to navigate to other images whose thumbnails cannot be seen. Click and drag just beneath the scroll bar area to resize the thumbnail browser. You can also choose to hide the thumbnail browser by clicking View, Thumbnails, and then Hide in the main menu.

● Enter Full Screen

You can edit a photograph in full-screen mode by clicking the Enter full screen button (). The image appears against a black background with the thumbnail browser hidden at the top of the screen and the toolbar hidden at the bottom of the screen. When you position the mouse pointer () over the top or bottom of the screen, the thumbnail browser or the toolbar appears, respectively. To exit full-screen mode you can click the Exit full screen button () or press the Esc key on the keyboard.

● Rotate, Crop, Straighten

The Rotate (), Crop (), and Straighten () buttons enable you to manipulate the geometry of photographs, as well as crop images to various dimensions and straighten crooked photos. These tools enable you to correct those not-so-perfect photographs for a more professional look.

● Enhance, Red-Eye, Retouch

The Enhance (), Red-Eye (), and Retouch () buttons give you the opportunity to fix some of the most common photographic problems with a simple click. Instantly adjust levels such as Saturation and Shadows for more pleasing photographs by clicking the Enhance tool. Reduce the red-eye from a portrait with the Red-Eye tool, or, using the Retouch tool, click or drag over a skin blemish in a photograph to remove it.

● Effects

The Effects window () can give your photographs a unique touch by adding effects such as Black and White, Sepia, and Antique. Effects such as Edge Blur and Boost Color can create some eye-catching effects.

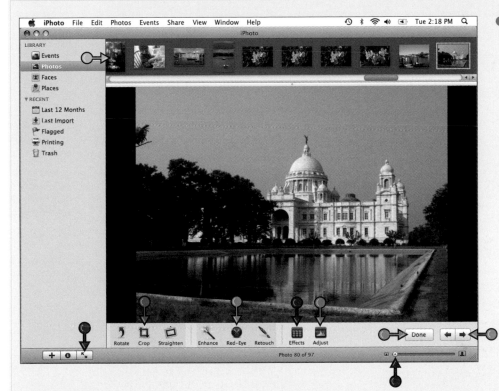

● **Adjust**

The Adjust window (⊞) enables you to fine-tune the aesthetic value of your photographs by adjusting aspects of the image such as exposure, color balance, highlights, and shadows. The Adjust Window is a convenient way to improve your images at the channel level. When you click the Enhance tool you can see adjustments automatically made to sliders within the Adjust window. The Adjust window enables you to tweak these settings manually to your own liking.

● **Done**

You can save every edit that you have made to an image by clicking Done. When you make changes to your photos, the edits will be reflected in every instance of the photo within albums, slideshows, photo books, calendars, and cards.

● **Save Changes, Move to Next Photo in Edit View**

When you click these buttons, all of the changes that you have made to the current image are saved, and iPhoto progresses to the next photo in the group, or the previous photo.

● **Change Size of Photos**

You can zoom into the image being displayed in the main Edit view window by dragging this slider. As you drag the slider, the Navigation window opens in the main viewing area, showing where you have zoomed into the image. Drag inside of the navigation window to pinpoint an area of the photo to zoom into.

When you edit in full screen the image is magnified to fit the entire screen and you have the advantage of a bigger image and a black background for less color distraction. You still have access to the thumbnail browser as well as the toolbar in full screen mode, but they stay hidden until you roll the mouse pointer ( ) over the areas so they do not occupy precious screen real estate. Editing in full screen is beneficial when you need as much clarity and detail as possible.

Edit In Full Screen

1 Click the photo you want to edit.

2 Click the **Enter Full Screen** button ( ).

The image is magnified to fill the computer screen.

3 Position the to the bottom of the screen.

The iPhoto edit tools appear.

④ Click the **Move to the Next Photo in Full Screen Mode** arrow (■) to view the next photo in the folder.

You can now edit the next photo in the group.

Note: Position the ⬉ to the top of the screen to reveal the photo browser and jump between nonconsecutive photos.

⑤ Click ⊠.

Note: You can also press **Esc** *to exit full screen.*

Can I compare my edited photo to another in the group at full screen?

Yes. You can do a side-by-side comparison of photos while in full screen mode by following these steps:

① Repeat Steps **1** to **3** to edit a photo full screen.

② Click **Compare** (○) and the next image in the group appears side by side with the current photo being edited.

Rotate Photos

In a photo where the subject may be sideways or upside down, iPhoto enables you to rotate photos right side up. A photo can be rotated clockwise or counterclockwise.

Rotate Photos

① Click the photo that you want to rotate.

② Click the **Edit** button (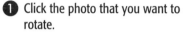).

iPhoto opens the photo in Edit view.

③ Click the **Rotate** button ().

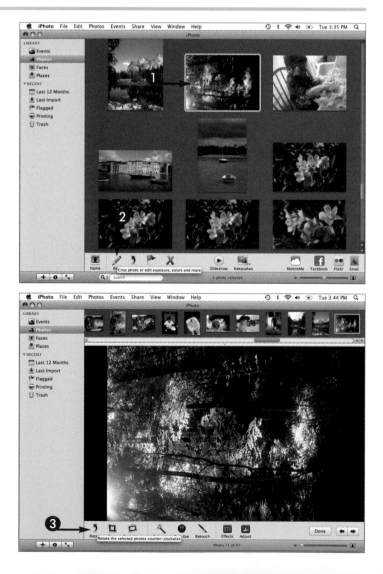

iPhoto rotates the image 90 degrees counterclockwise.

④ Repeat Step **3** until the image is right side up.

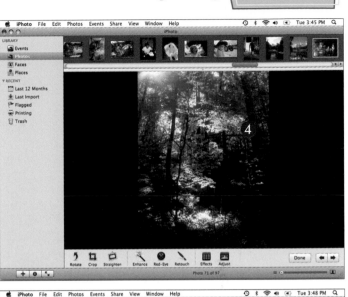

⑤ Click **Done**.

iPhoto exits Edit mode.

TIP

Can I rotate an image clockwise?

Yes. You can press and hold Option on the keyboard and the Rotate button changes from counterclockwise (🔄) to clockwise (🔄). With Option held down, click the clockwise **Rotate** button (🔄) to rotate the image clockwise by 90 degrees. You can also Control-click the image and choose **Rotate Clockwise** from the menu. If you feel that you need clockwise more often than counterclockwise, just change it in iPhoto's General preference pane.

Straighten Photos

If you have a crooked photo, you can use iPhoto to straighten the photo clockwise or counterclockwise for a level photograph.

❶ Click the image that you want to straighten.

❷ Click the **Edit** button (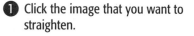).

The photo opens in Edit view.

❸ Click the **Straighten** button ().

iPhoto displays a grid over the photo.

④ Drag the slider to the left to decrease the angle counterclockwise.

⑤ Click **Done**.

iPhoto exits Edit view.

TIP

How can I tell when the photo is level?
You can use the grid lines that appear over the photo once you begin to straighten the photo. Locate a horizontally aligned feature within the photo and begin to straighten so that the feature is parallel with the nearest horizontal line grid. You can also use a vertical feature in the photo and straighten it in reference to a vertical line in the grid.

Crop to Enhance Your Photos

You can improve a photo by reframing the composition of the shot to remove unwanted areas. Cropping is a great way to correct shot composition and can help focus and emphasize the main subject of a shot.

① Click the photo that you want to crop.

② Click the **Edit** button ().

iPhoto displays the editing tools.

③ Click the **Crop** button ( ).

iPhoto displays the cropping rectangle over the photo.

④ Click and drag the top, bottom, corners, or sides of the rectangle to frame the composition of the photo.

⑤ Click **Apply**.

iPhoto saves the cropped photo.

⑥ Click **Done**.

iPhoto exits Edit mode.

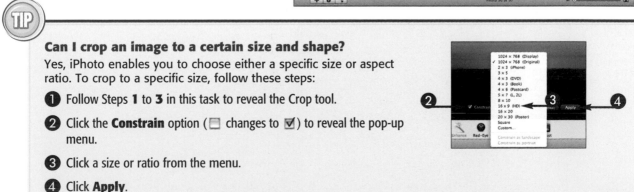

TIP

Can I crop an image to a certain size and shape?
Yes, iPhoto enables you to choose either a specific size or aspect ratio. To crop to a specific size, follow these steps:

① Follow Steps **1** to **3** in this task to reveal the Crop tool.

② Click the **Constrain** option (☐ changes to ☑) to reveal the pop-up menu.

③ Click a size or ratio from the menu.

④ Click **Apply**.

Prepare Photos for Use in iMovie

You can prepare your photos for use in video projects that you create in iMovie by using the Crop tool. Use the 16x9 (HD), 4x3 (DVD), and Custom crop settings in iPhoto to ensure that your photos match the aspect ratio of your video projects. HD can be either 1280x720 (720p) or 1920x1080 (1080i and 1080p). For the US and other locations that use NTSC, SD should be 640x480. PAL is 720x586.

Prepare Photos for Use in iMovie

① Click the photo that you want to crop.

② Click the **Edit** button (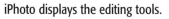).

iPhoto displays the editing tools.

③ Click the **Crop** button ().

iPhoto displays the cropping rectangle over the photo.

④ Click the **Constrain** option (☐ changes to ☑) and choose a dimension that matches your video project, 16x9 (HD) or 4x3 (DVD).

A white box of the chosen dimension appears around the photo and the Constrain box is checked.

⑤ Move the crop box around the image and frame the shot within the specified dimensions.

iPhoto constrains the dimensions to the specified cropping dimension.

⑥ Click **Apply**.

TIP

How do I create a photo at a customized dimension?
You can create an image at a custom dimension by choosing **Custom** from the crop menu. Type in a custom dimension and then click **Apply**.

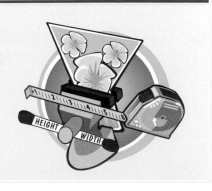

You can remove small blemishes and marks within photos using the Retouch tool. Retouching an image in iPhoto can help you remove minor unwanted imperfections, and can be done with a few simple clicks.

1 Click the photo that you want to retouch.

2 Click the **Edit** button (📝).

iPhoto displays the editing tools.

3 Click the **Retouch** button (🖊).

The Retouch controls appear.

4 Drag the slider (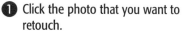) to pick a brush size for the area you are retouching.

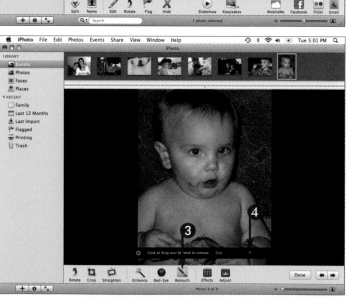

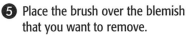

5 Place the brush over the blemish that you want to remove.

6 Click repeatedly or drag across the area to remove the blemish.

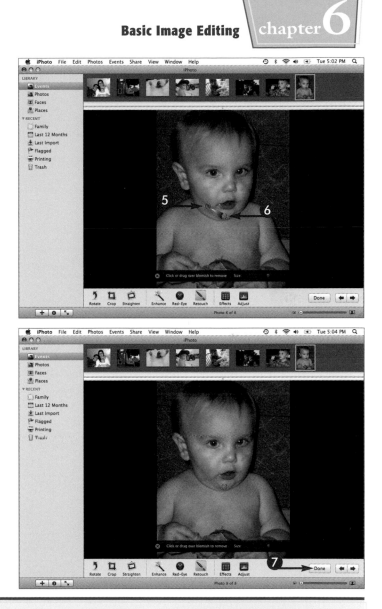

Note: For a quick comparison, press Shift *to toggle between before and after views.*

7 Click **Done**.

iPhoto exits Edit mode.

Are there any retouching techniques that could help me?
Yes. If the affected area with the blemish is small, use a smaller brush size and continue to click the area, as opposed to dragging it, until the blemish is gone. If the area is large, use a larger brush size and try dragging over the blemish to blend it into the surrounding areas of the image.

Using the Enhance Button

A quick way to instantly improve the appearance of a photo is to use the Enhance button. With a simple click of the Enhance button, iPhoto analyzes the brightness of the photo and attempts to perform a color balance by lightening or darkening the photo, raising the contrast, and boosting dull colors.

Use the Enhance Button

① Click the image that you want to enhance.

② Click the **Edit** button (⊿).

iPhoto opens the photo in Edit view.

③ Click the **Enhance** button (⬚).

Note: *You can also press* Control *and click the photo and then click* **Enhance** *from the menu.*

④ Click **Done** to return to the previous view and pick a new photo.

● You can choose another photo to enhance.

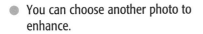

TIP

What if I do not like the result after using the Enhance tool?
When you use the Enhance tool, iPhoto uses algorithms to take an educated guess as to how to improve the image. You can always adjust the parameters manually in the Adjust window. For photos that you are initially unsure how to improve, open the Adjust window and then click the **Enhance** button to get yourself started. You are able to see the parameters automatically adjust in the Adjust window, and can then tweak away.

Red-eye is a common photographic anomaly that occurs when the camera's flash reflects off of the back of the subject's eyes, causing the eyes to glow red. You can use the Red-Eye tool to help reduce this unwanted effect.

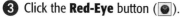

① Click the image that contains the red-eye.

② Click the **Edit** button ( ).

iPhoto opens the photo in Edit view.

③ Click the **Red-Eye** button ( ).

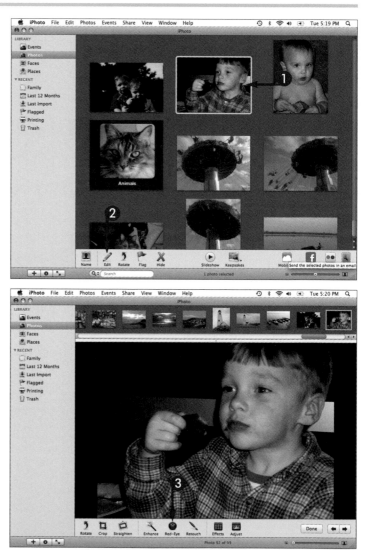

The Red-Eye controls appear.

Note: You can use the size slider in the Red-Eye controls to increase the size of the photo for this procedure.

 Click **Auto**.

iPhoto detects faces in the photo and reduces the red-eye.

 Click **Done**.

iPhoto exits Edit view.

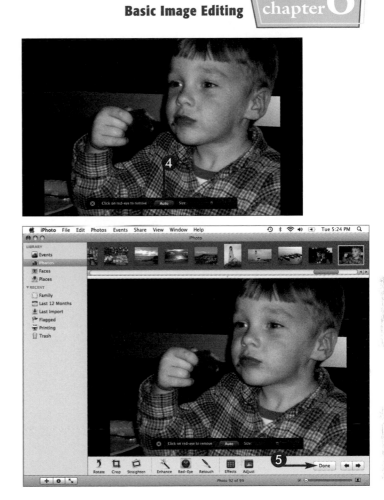

iPhoto does not remove the red-eye when I click Auto in the Red-Eye controls?

It is quite possible that the red is not red enough to be effectively removed automatically with the iPhoto Red-Eye tool. You may have to manually remove the red-eye. Follow these steps to manually remove red-eye:

① Follow Steps **1** to **3** to display the Red-Eye controls.

② Drag the size slider in the Red-Eye controls to match the red-eye in the photo.

③ Click the eye that contains red to correct the color.

④ Repeat Steps **2** and **3** to remove all instances of red-eye in the photo.

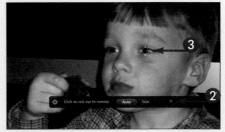

CHAPTER 7

Enhancing Your Photos

iPhoto provides a variety of sophisticated photo processing tools that are easy to use. You can transform less than perfect photos into eye-catching works of art by learning to use the Adjust tools such as the Exposure and Contrast sliders, as well as the Highlights, Shadows, and De-noise sliders. All enhancements performed in iPhoto are non-destructive, so you can try out effects, while still being able to revert back to the original photo. iPhoto also gives you added flexibility while enhancing photos by allowing you to use high-quality RAW files.

Tour of the Adjust Window

The Adjust window enables you to enhance the aesthetic value of your photographs by adjusting aspects of the image with sliders. You can fine-tune exposure, tweak color balance, adjust highlights and shadows, and more in the Adjust window. Knowing your way around the Adjust window can help you produce higher quality photographs. Any adjustment that you make to a photo in the Adjust window changes the appearance of that photo in every album, slideshow, book, calendar, and card.

Histogram

The histogram represents the distribution of a photo's tonal values such as blacks and whites and everything in between. The Levels sliders under the histogram enable you to specify what iPhoto considers to be pure black or pure white. The histogram and the Levels sliders can help you achieve proper exposure and contrast in photographs.

Levels

The Levels sliders are a great way to adjust both brightness and contrast in an image. These three sliders can be used independently or in conjunction with the Exposure slider to improve exposure and contrast. When you use the Levels sliders, iPhoto stretches the existing tonal range of the image. Keep a close eye on the histogram display while adjusting the Levels sliders.

Exposure

The Exposure slider adjusts the overall brightness of the image. The Exposure slider can be used independently or in conjunction with the Levels sliders to improve exposure and contrast in photographs. Keep a close eye on the histogram display while adjusting the Exposure slider.

Contrast

The Contrast slider increases or decreases the difference between light and dark areas in a photo. The Contrast slider affects the contrast range of the entire image.

Saturation

You can increase or decrease the intensity of colors in a photo with the Saturation slider. You can use the Saturation slider to create color effects by increasing color vibrancy in a photo, creating a black and white image, or fading colors.

Definition

The Definition slider adjusts contrast for only specific parts of the image, as opposed to the entire image, like the Contrast slider. Use the Definition slider to reduce haze in photographs and improve overall picture clarity.

Highlights and Shadows

These two sliders enable you to adjust both highlights and shadows in an image independently. Use these two sliders to reveal more detail in areas of the photos that were originally too dark or too bright.

● Sharpness

The Sharpness slider enables you to adjust the noise definition of a photograph and make images appear crisper. You can use the Sharpness slider to make intricate textures in subjects stand out in a photograph.

● De-noise

The De-noise slider can help reduce the digital noise found in low-light or high-ISO photographs. Digital noise in photographs generally occurs in areas with little detail, such as a clear, blue sky.

● Temperature

You can use the Temperature slider to adjust the tones in a photograph between cool and warm. Cool tones used in a photograph taken of a city street corner could help you portray the grit of the city, whereas warmer tones in a photo taken at the beach can portray a tropical paradise.

● Tint

The Tint slider enables you to create overall color casts in photographs, ranging from red to green, to create interesting effects. Moving the slider to the right gives the photo a magenta tint, as red and blue are added to the image. Moving the slider to the right gives the photo a green tint. The adjustment made with the Tint slider can be dramatic, so use it judiciously.

● Eyedropper

Use the eyedropper button to reduce unwanted color casts due to improper white balancing. When the eyedropper is selected, you can click a part of the image that is supposed to be white or gray, to perform a color balance. Color balancing ensures that whites and light grays are portrayed correctly in photographs.

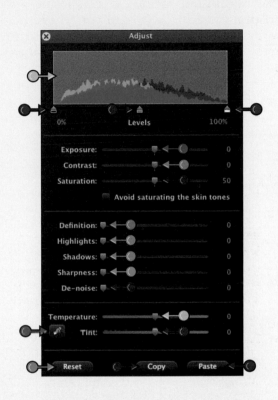

● Reset

Click the Reset button to return all of the parameters in the Adjust window to their default values.

● Copy and Paste Buttons

The Copy and Paste buttons save you a lot of time by enabling you to copy Adjust window parameters and paste them to other photographs.

Understanding the Histogram

The histogram is a live update that displays the light and dark values in a photograph such as blacks and whites as well as midtones. Pure black is represented on the left side of the histogram and pure white on the right. Midtones are represented in the middle. The iPhoto histogram breaks down the tonal data of an image into the primary colors: red, green, and blue. Understanding the histogram can help you adjust for proper exposure and contrast.

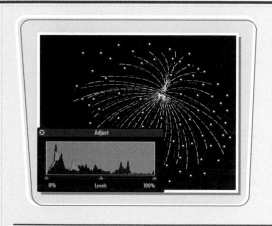

Darker Photos and the Histogram

The darker shades of the photograph appear on the left the histogram. If you have a picture that was shot in low light or in a shaded area, peaks appear to the left side of the histogram and quickly taper off to the right.

Lighter Photos and the Histogram

The lighter shades of the photograph appear on the right side of the histogram. If you have a picture that is primarily light, like a picture of a snow-covered hillside on a sunny day, most of the tonal information appears to the right of the histogram in the form of peaks.

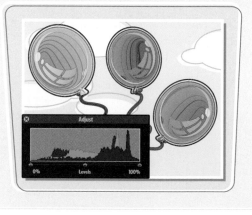

Well-Balanced Photo and the Histogram

Most well-balanced shots have data spread throughout the entire histogram, with the occasional peak here and there.

Exposure Problems and the Histogram

A photo that has been improperly exposed, underexposed (too dark), or overexposed (too light) displays sharp peaks at either the extreme left or right of the histogram. Severely over- and underexposed shots lose precious picture information (detail) in the extreme dark or light areas of the image. To correct the image, you need to use the Adjust window to spread the peaks and values throughout the histogram.

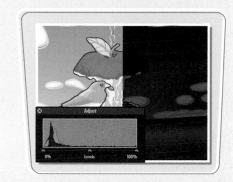

Three Superimposed Channels

The histogram breaks down the tonal data of an image into the primary colors: red, green, and blue. These channels are graphed on top of one another in the histogram. When you move the Exposure slider to make adjustments to brightness, all three channels move together and either become bunched together, if you move the slider to the left, or spread out, if you move the slider to the right. Either way, the three superimposed graphs primarily keep the same shape and move together. When you start to manipulate color parameters, such as Saturation and Temperature, red, green, and blue channels begin to move independently.

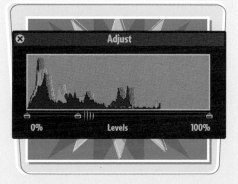

Using the Levels

If there are peaks and valleys spread from left to right throughout the histogram, the picture more than likely has a good color balance. If the histogram displays sharp peaks to the left or right, with very few peaks and valleys throughout the rest of the graph, you may want to consider making adjustments by moving either the left or right levels inward. Moving the right level inward makes the highlights brighter, whereas the dark areas stay mostly the same. Moving the right level inward changes the dark tones while the bright areas of the image remain mostly unaffected. After the endpoints have been adjusted, move the center level to adjust the midtones. A good rule of thumb is to adjust the center slider to where it is centered between the left and right levels. This generally results in a pleasing image, but feel free to adjust to your own personal satisfaction.

Adjust Exposure and Contrast

iPhoto enables you to adjust the lightness or darkness of a photo to achieve proper balance. You can also increase or decrease the contrast between the lightest parts of the image and the darkest parts of the image for more dramatic photos. Correcting exposure and tweaking contrast can make for more compelling photographs.

Adjust Exposure and Contrast

① Click the photo you want to adjust.

② Click the **Edit** button (🖉).

iPhoto opens the photo in Edit view.

③ Click the **Adjust** button (🔲).

The Adjust window appears.

④ Drag the **Exposure** slider to the left to make the picture darker or to the right to make it lighter, depending on the photograph.

The picture in the viewing area becomes lighter or darker.

⑤ Drag the **Contrast** slider to the right to make dark areas darker and light areas lighter, or to the left to make light and dark areas lighter.

You can see the changes to contrast in the viewing area and histogram.

Note: Pushing peaks outside the edges of the histogram can sometimes result in the loss of precious data in light and dark areas when you print the image.

⑥ Click **Done** to return to the previous view and pick a new photo.

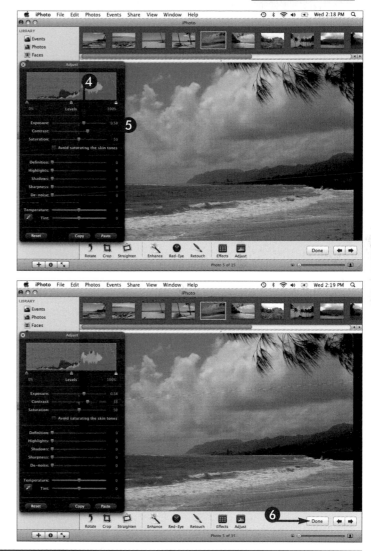

TIPS

After I make my adjustment can I see a before and after?

Yes. You can see a quick before and after of the image by pressing and releasing **Shift** on the keyboard. The picture in the viewing area toggles between the original and the edited image.

What if I do not like my changes and want to start over.

Click **Reset** at the bottom of the Adjust window to restore the parameters back to their default state and undo the adjustments.

Adjust Highlights and Shadows

The Highlights slider and the Shadows slider can be used to recover detail in the darkest and brightest areas of the image. The Highlights slider darkens the brightest part of the image, whereas the Shadows slider lightens the darkest parts of the image, to reveal details that were once lost. You can use both of these sliders to improve overall detail in a photo.

① Click the photo that you want to adjust.

② Click the **Edit** button (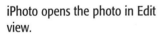).

iPhoto opens the photo in Edit view.

③ Click the **Adjust** button (📊).

The Adjust window appears.

④ Drag the **Highlights** slider to darken the lightest parts the image.

⑤ Drag the **Shadows** slider to lighten the darkest parts of the image.

Note: Dragging the Shadows slider too far to the left can result in a strange effect on the image.

⑥ Click **Done**.

iPhoto returns to the previous view so you can pick a new photo.

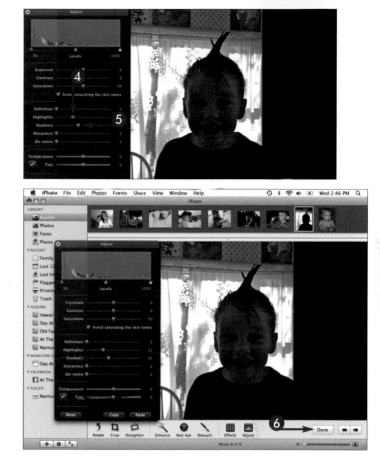

How can I undo the last three changes that I made to the image without resetting everything?

You can undo changes by following these steps:

① Click **Edit**.

② Click **Undo**.

③ Repeat Steps **1** and **2** two more times to undo changes.

Can I copy my adjustments to other photographs?

Yes. Follow these steps:

① After you make the adjustments in the Adjust window, click **Copy**.

② Select another photo and click **Paste**.

Balance the Colors

iPhoto can help you fix common photographic mistakes, such as taking a shot with an improper white balance. An improper white balance can lead to unwanted color casts in your photographs such as a slightly orange or blue image. These unwanted color casts are due to the camera's misrepresentation of neutral colors. The iPhoto eyedropper can help you fix images with unwanted color casts by adjusting colors in the photos so that whites appear white and light grays appear correctly.

Color Balance

Balance the Colors

① Click the image that you want to edit.

② Click the **Edit** button (✐).

iPhoto opens the photo in Edit view.

③ Click the **Adjust** button (▣).

The Adjust window appears.

④ Click the **Eyedropper** button ( ).

● A message prompts you to pick a neutral gray or white point in the photo to remove the color cast.

⑤ Position the pointer over an area in the photo closest to the correct representation of white or gray in the image.

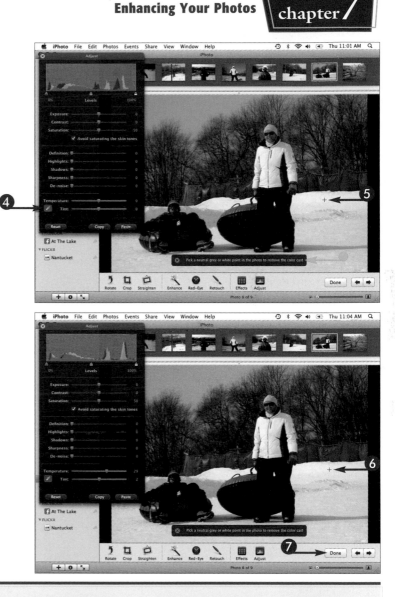

⑥ Click the color in the photograph.

iPhoto automatically adjusts the photo's tint and temperature.

⑦ Click **Done**.

TIPS

How do I keep iPhoto from changing the color of every instance of a particular photo in iPhoto when I make adjustments?

When you make a change to a photo in the Adjust window, every instance of that photo in iPhoto reflects those changes. To change only a single instance you must make a duplicate photo before you edit. Press Control on the keyboard and click the image you want to edit, then choose **Duplicate** from the menu. Perform the edit on the duplicate photo.

I do not like the result when I use the eyedropper. What else can I do?

If you do not like the auto adjustment achieved by the eyedropper, you can manually tweak the **Temperature** slider and **Tint** slider in the Adjust window.

Enhance Colors

The iPhoto Adjust window provides a number of ways for you to improve and enhance colors in a photo. The Saturation, Temperature, and Tint sliders can help you create warm vivid colors in your photographs.

Enhance Colors

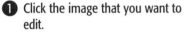

① Click the image that you want to edit.

② Click the **Edit** button ().

iPhoto opens the photo in Edit view.

③ Click the **Adjust** button ().

The Adjust window appears.

Note: You can use either Step 4, 5, or 6 to enhance colors, or a combination of them.

④ Drag the **Saturation** slider to the right to increase the richness of the colors.

⑤ Drag the **Temperature** slider to the right for warmer color temperatures.

⑥ Drag the **Tint** slider to add a color cast to the photo.

⑦ Click **Done** to return to the previous screen and pick a new image.

 TIPS

I increased the saturation in the Adjust window, but when I print the photograph, why are the colors not as vivid?

Your Mac computer screen has a wider color range than a printer does. If you increase the saturation too much, you will not be able to reproduce what you see on screen in a print.

What can I do to improve an older, scanned image that has turned reddish yellow.

You can drag the **Temperature** slider to the left to remove some of the red and yellow from the older image.

Apply Effects to a Photo

You can enhance a photo and give it a unique look by applying an effect. iPhoto offers a variety of effects such as B&W (black and white), Sepia, Antique, Fade Color, Boost Color, Matte, Vignette, and Edge Blur.

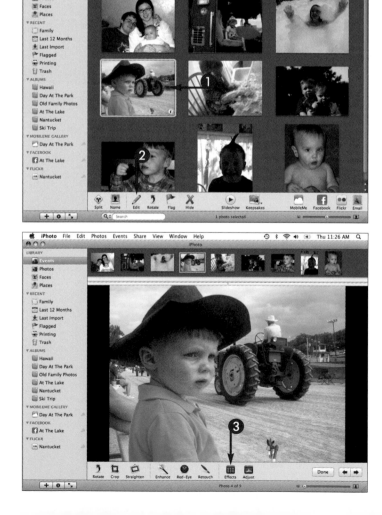

① Click the photo that you want to enhance.

② Click the **Edit** button ().

iPhoto displays the editing tools.

③ Click the **Effects** button (▦).

iPhoto displays the Effects window.

④ Click the effect you want to apply.

iPhoto applies the effect.

⑤ If the effect offers a numerical value, click the arrows to adjust the effect.

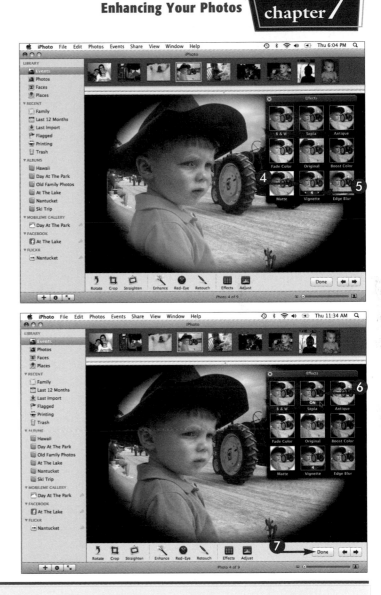

⑥ Repeat Step **4** to add more effects to the photo.

⑦ Click **Done**.

iPhoto exits Edit mode.

TIPS

Is there a way to improve the look of my original photo without effects?

Yes. The **Enhance** tool optimizes exposure, contrast, and color saturation along with other values at the click of a button. Click the photo that you want to enhance, click **Edit**, and then click the **Enhance** tool ( ) to improve the image. You also have the option to click **Adjust** and manually adjust these values for the image.

How do I remove effects?

If the effect you have applied has a numeric value, you can click the arrow to set the effect value to **0** to remove the effect. If the effect you have applied does not have a numeric value, but an On state, click the effect again in the Effects window to toggle off the effect. If you have applied multiple effects to an image, right-click the image and choose **Revert to Previous**.

Adjust Sharpness

All digital images have an inherent softness, and iPhoto gives you control over the perceived sharpness of your photographs. An image with plenty of detail can be a prime candidate for sharpening to accentuate its intricacies. Portraits may benefit from a softening of the image to hide less-than-perfect skin detail.

Adjust Sharpness

① Click the image that you want to edit.

② Click the **Edit** button (✏️).

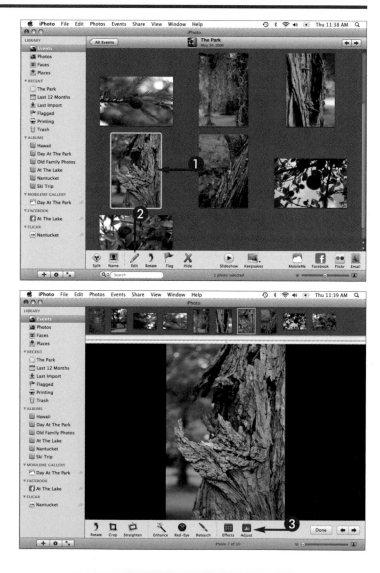

iPhoto opens the photo in Edit view.

③ Click the **Adjust** button (▦).

The Adjust window appears.

④ Drag the **Sharpness** slider to the right to increase sharpness or drag it to the left to soften the image.

Note: Generally, sharpening should be the last adjustment that you make in the Adjust window. If you sharpen the image first, then make further edits in the Adjust window, you may find yourself having to sharpen the image again.

⑤ Click **Done** to return to the previous view and pick a new photo.

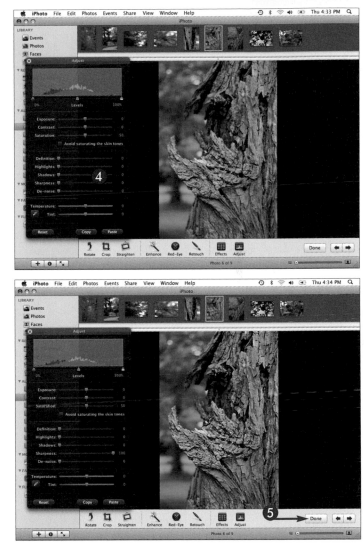

 TIPS

Why does my photograph look very grainy after sharpening?

iPhoto increases the contrast between light and dark pixels in order to give the illusion of sharpening to an image. Increasing the sharpness too much can ruin a photo because the pixels increasingly become grainy. Use increased sharpening sparingly.

When should I sharpen a photo?

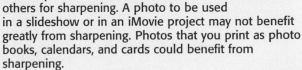

This question is very subjective and depends largely on the photographer and the photo in question. With that being said, there are some pictures that may be better candidates than others for sharpening. A photo to be used in a slideshow or in an iMovie project may not benefit greatly from sharpening. Photos that you print as photo books, calendars, and cards could benefit from sharpening.

Reduce Noise

Grain, or digital noise, is a common problem in digital photography when shooting in low light or with a cheap digital camera. If a photo is grainy, you can use the De-noise slider in iPhoto to reduce the noise for a more pleasing photograph.

Reduce Noise

① Click the image that you want to edit.

② Click the **Edit** button (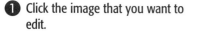).

iPhoto opens the photo in Edit view.

③ Click the **Adjust** button (🖼).

The Adjust window opens.

④ Drag the **Size** slider () to magnify the image.

The Navigation box automatically opens in the window.

Note: *You can also magnify the image by 100 or 200 percent by pressing ① or ②.*

⑤ Use the Navigation box to pinpoint a dark segment of the photo.

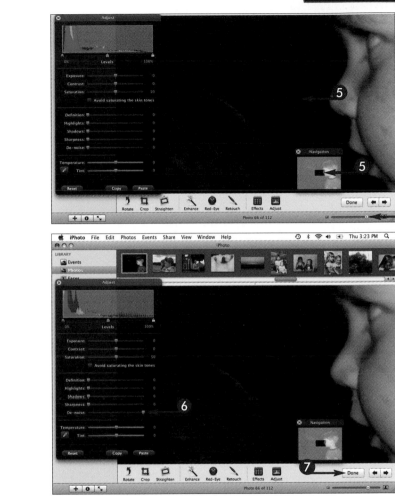

Note: *Zooming into a dark segment of the picture, where most of the noise is present, helps you to gauge how much to move the De-noise slider. The noise is reduced by the blurring of pixels, so be mindful of how much you blur a photograph.*

⑥ Drag the **De-noise** slider to the right to reduce the grain of the image.

⑦ Click **Done**.

iPhoto returns to the previous view.

TIPS

How do I remove all changes made to a photograph globally in iPhoto?

Edits you make to images in iPhoto do not change the original instance of the photo on your computer hard drive. To revert a photograph back to its original state, press Control on the keyboard and click the image. Click **Revert to Previous** from the menu.

> Next
> Previous
>
> Edit Using Full Screen
> Edit in External Editor
>
> Rotate Clockwise
> Rotate Counter Clockwise
>
> Show Info
>
> Duplicate
> Reset
> **Revert to Original** ◄

How do I remove all changes made to a RAW-format photograph in iPhoto.

You can revert RAW-format photos back to their original state by clicking **Photos** and then clicking **Reprocess RAW**.

> Next
> Previous
>
> Edit Using Full Screen
> Edit in External Editor
>
> Rotate Clockwise
> Rotate Counter Clockwise
>
> Show Info
>
> Duplicate
> Reset
> **Reprocess RAW** ◄

When shooting photos in the JPEG format, the camera compresses the image so that it takes up less space on the memory card, in turn sacrificing image quality and some processing flexibility. When you shoot in the RAW format, you get the original, uncompressed image data as recorded by the light sensor. RAW files contain significantly more picture information than do JPEG files, and in turn, require more storage space and more processing time on the computer. Working with RAW files provides you a higher-quality image with more flexibility to edit in iPhoto.

How Do I Shoot RAW?

Many midrange cameras and practically all high-end cameras have the ability to shoot in the RAW format. In order to shoot in the RAW format you have to go into your camera's menu system. Typically, you can find the RAW option in the Mode or Image Quality menu of the camera.

Are You Compatible?

Camera manufacturers create their own flavor of RAW format. Even though your camera has the ability to shoot in the RAW format and iPhoto accepts RAW files, iPhoto still may not be compatible with your camera's particular RAW format. The current address on Apple's Web site for supported cameras is www.apple.com/aperture/specs/raw.html. It is a page dedicated to Apple's Aperture software, but the cameras listed are also compatible with iPhoto.

More Space Required

Because RAW files are uncompressed they take up more space, which means you cannot store as many RAW files on a memory card as you could JPEG files. An 8-megapixel JPEG file may take up 4MB of space whereas the RAW file may use 16MB. You will need to invest in more memory cards to store the same number of RAW files as JPEG files. Keep the RAW format space requirements in mind when purchasing hard drive space.

More Time Required

RAW files take longer to transfer from your camera to your Mac. This is largely due to some of the extra processing that needs to take place. By and large, iPhoto was designed to work with JPEG files. Upon transferring RAW files from your camera, iPhoto creates a JPEG version of the RAW files. So, when you are working with RAW files in iPhoto, you are essentially viewing and editing JPEG files. When you make edits to the RAW file and click **Done**, iPhoto updates the RAW image data and saves it as a JPEG file, while the original RAW file remains untouched on the hard drive.

The Advantages of JPEG Representation

When iPhoto imports a RAW file from the camera and creates a JPEG representation of the RAW file, iPhoto enables you to work with the uncompressed files as easily as you would the JPEG files, without the frustrating processing times. Also, the JPEG version enables you to use the photographs you shot in the RAW format, in programs that do not support the RAW format such as iDVD, iMovie, and iWeb.

The RAW Advantage

When you shoot in the RAW format, you get the original, uncompressed image data and you are not limited to the color, exposure, and sharpness dictated by camera compression. The inherent advantage of editing RAW files in iPhoto is that you begin with a higher-quality image that contains more image data than the JPEG files, which enables you to make dramatic changes while editing images. iPhoto '09 also has improved support for RAW format photos.

Access Advanced RAW Format Options

iPhoto enables you to save your edited RAW files to high-quality, uncompressed TIFF files, instead of JPEG files, or edit RAW files in a more sophisticated external photo editor like Adobe Photoshop.

Access Advanced Raw Format Options

SAVE EDITED RAW FILES AS TIFF FILES

① Click **iPhoto** in the main menu.

② Click **Preferences**.

The iPhoto Preferences open.

③ Click **Advanced**.

④ Select the **Save edits as 16-bit TIFF files** check box (☐ changes to ☑).

Now when iPhoto saves edits to RAW files it saves them as high-quality, uncompressed TIFF files instead of the lossy JPEG format.

Note: *The saved TIFF files are much larger than the JPEG file. The 16-bit TIFF files provide you more flexibility when performing dramatic edits to brightness levels.*

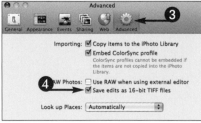

USE AN EXTERNAL EDITOR

① Click **iPhoto**.

② Click **Preferences**.

The iPhoto Preferences open.

③ Click **Advanced**.

④ Select the **Use RAW when using external editor** check box (□ changes to ☑).

⑤ Close the Preferences.

Now, when you Control -click the RAW file and choose **Edit in External Editor**, the photo opens in the designated editor.

How can I take advantage of the improved support for RAW files in iPhoto '09 with photos originally imported into iPhoto 6 or earlier?

You can select one or more RAW-format photos taken in iPhoto 6 or earlier, click Photos and then click Reprocess RAW to take advantage of the improved support for RAW-format photos. All previous edits to the RAW-format photo are overwritten. The improvements include clearer detail, deeper color, and improved highlights.

Showcasing
Your Photos

Slideshows are a great way to showcase your photos in iPhoto. You can create a quick slideshow to review newly imported photographs or design highly polished slideshows with customized motion effects that you can save. iPhoto enables you to create QuickTime-compatible slideshow movies and even burn CDs and DVDs of photo projects.

Create a Temporary Slideshow

You can create a temporary slideshow with a theme, music, and transitions from an event, album, book, or group of photos. Creating a temporary slideshow is a quick way to preview a newly imported group of pictures without creating a slideshow project in the Source list.

① In the iPhoto Source list, click a collection of photos to view as a temporary slideshow.

② Click the **Slideshow** button ().

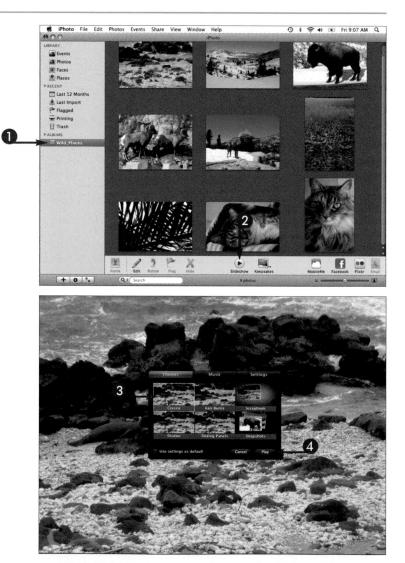

A dialog appears prompting you to pick a theme. To see a preview of each theme, you can position the mouse pointer (▶) over the thumbnail.

Note: All six of the slideshow options use face detection to keep faces on-screen.

③ Choose a theme.

④ Click **Play**.

The slideshow plays in full screen with the default theme music.

Create a Saved Slideshow

You can create a slideshow of any selected event, album, book, or group of photos and have it appear in the Source list. Having the slideshow appear in the Source list enables you to return to the slideshow later. Seeing your photos as a full-screen slideshow with music is a great way to present your photos to your friends.

Create a Saved Slideshow

① In the Source list, click a collection of photos to view as a slideshow.

② Click the **Plus** button (➕).

iPhoto displays a dialog.

③ Click **Slideshow**.

④ Type a name.

⑤ Click **Create**.

● iPhoto displays the slideshow in the Source list.

● You can preview the slideshow in the Photo Viewing area by clicking the **Preview** button (⬛).

⑥ Click the **Play** button (▶) to watch the slideshow.

iPhoto plays the slideshow at the default settings and music.

Add iTunes Music to a Slideshow

You can choose the song that plays during the slideshow. Being able to select your own music track is a great way to personalize your photo presentation.

Add iTunes Music to a Slideshow

① At the bottom of the iPhoto photo viewing window, click the **Music** button ().

The Music Settings dialog appears.

② Click the **Source** .

③ Click **iTunes** from the pop-up menu.

Note: You can also click an iTunes playlist to specify a series of songs that play during a long slideshow.

④ Click the song you want to use.

● You can preview the song before adding to the slideshow by clicking the **Play** button () in the Music Settings dialog.

⑤ Click **Apply**.

6 Click the **Play** button 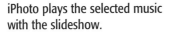.

iPhoto plays the selected music
with the slideshow.

How do I change the order of my photos and add new photos to the slideshow?

You can rearrange the order of the photos appearing in your
slideshow by dragging and dropping photos in the photo browser at
the top of the iPhoto viewing area. Add new photos by dragging them
directly onto the slideshow project in the Source list.

View Saved Slideshow Settings

You have many options for customizing slideshow presentations of photographs in iPhoto. You can specify settings that affect the overall slideshow, including the duration of slides on-screen, transition type, and whether captions are shown. You can even specify unique settings for individual slides. The ability to customize your own slideshow presentation enables you to add a personal touch to how your photographs are showcased.

● All Slides

The All Slides option enables you to change the settings of the slideshow as a whole. Click All Slides to make overall adjustments to slideshows.

● Play each slide for a minimum of 5 seconds

Specify how long each slide appears on-screen by clicking the radio button and then clicking the arrow buttons to increase or decrease the time.

● Fit slideshow to music

Click the radio button so that the duration of slides is adjusted to make the show play as long as the music you choose.

● Transition

Click the Transition check box and choose a transition effect from the pop-up menu.

● Speed

Change how fast the transition effect occurs between photographs in the slideshow by dragging the Speed bar.

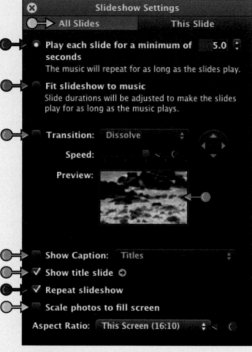

● Preview

You can preview the transition effect you have chosen in the Preview area.

● Show Caption

Click the Show Caption check box and then choose a caption from the pop-up menu that you want to display for each slide in the show. You can choose from: Titles, Descriptions, Titles and Descriptions, Places, and Dates.

● Show title slide

Click the Show title slide check box to make the title of the slideshow project appear on the first slide.

● Repeat slideshow

Click the Repeat title check box to automatically repeat the slideshow after it has completed.

● Scale photos to fill screen

Click the Scale Photos check box so that photographs that have not been cropped to fit the aspect ratio of your display are scaled to fit the screen with black borders.

● Aspect Ratio

Specify the device on which you will show the slideshow by choosing an option from the pop-up menu. The aspect ratio of the slideshow is adjusted to play back correctly on the chosen device.

Slideshow Settings for This Slide

The This Slide option enables you to make changes to individual slides in the show. Click This Slide to make unique adjustments to a single photograph in the slideshow. Use these options to create unique looks for individual slides in a presentation. Customizing specific slides allows you to add your own personal touch during the show.

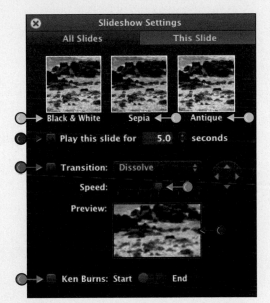

● **Effects**

Select an effect for an individual slide by clicking one of the thumbnails: Black & White, Sepia, or Antique. These particular effects can be used for customizing special effects. For example, you can have an individual slide fade from black and white into color, by placing duplicate photographs in succession in a slideshow and applying the B & W (black and white) effect to the first photograph.

● **Play this slide for**

Specify how long each slide appears on-screen by clicking the check box and then clicking the arrow buttons to increase or decrease the time. You can use this setting to establish a unique rhythm for your slideshow presentation.

● **Transition**

Click the Transition check box and choose a transition effect from the pop-up menu. You can use the Transition options to place a different transition between each slide in the presentation.

● **Speed**

Change how fast the transition effect occurs between photographs in the slideshow by dragging the Speed bar. Use this setting to customize the speed of transitions for added effect during the presentation.

● **Preview**

Preview the transition effect you have chosen in the Preview area before you begin the actual slideshow.

● **Ken Burns**

Click the check box to add motion to your slideshow projects and dictate the Start and End positions of the animation. The Ken Burns effect is a great way to bring still photos to life on-screen.

Using the Ken Burns Effect

iPhoto enables you to add motion to your photographs in a slideshow by allowing you to pan across images as well as zoom in and out, using the Ken Burns effect. You can use panning and zooming together to add depth to your photographs. The Ken Burns effect is available for Classic and Ken Burns slideshow themes and can be applied to all slides as well as individual slides.

Using the Ken Burns Effect

① Click a slideshow project in the Source list.

② Click the **Settings** button (⊞) to open the Slideshow Settings dialog.

③ Click the photo in the photo browser on which you want to apply the Ken Burns effect.

④ In the Slideshow Settings dialog, click **This Slide**.

The photo appears in the Settings pane as a thumbnail.

⑤ Click the **Ken Burns** check box (☐ changes to ☑).

⑥ Click **Start**.

⑦ Drag the **size slider** (⊡) to designate where the zoom begins.

⑧ Click the photo in the main iPhoto window.

The mouse pointer (↖) turns into a hand.

⑨ Drag the photo to the spot where you want the pan to begin.

⑩ Click **End**.

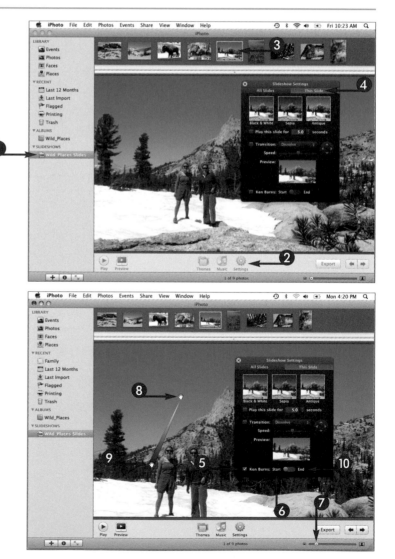

11 Drag the 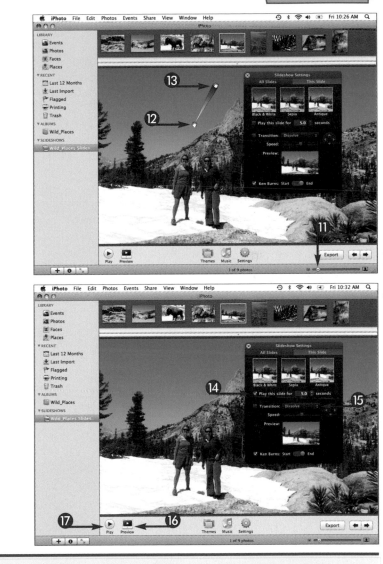 to designate where the zoom ends.

12 Click the photo in the main iPhoto window.

The ⬉ turns into a hand.

13 Drag the photo to the spot where you want the pan to end.

14 Click the **Play this slide for** check box (☐ changes to ☑).

15 Click the arrows to specify how long slides appear on-screen.

Note: The shorter the duration, the faster the pan or zoom effect occurs.

16 Click 🔲 to review the effect and then make changes if needed.

17 Click ▶ to review the actual slideshow.

TIP

How do I turn off the Ken Burns effect after it has been applied to a photo?

Select the photo in the photo browser above the iPhoto viewing area, and then uncheck the Ken Burns check box (☑ changes to ☐). The pan and zoom motion that you created for the slide is then cancelled. iPhoto does not retain your pan and zoom specifications after you uncheck the Ken Burns check box.

Create Effects with Duplicate Photos

You can create some eye-catching effects by duplicating photos, sequencing them together in a slideshow, and adding an effect to one of the copies. For example, a photo can start out black and white, then gradually fade into color if the first instance of the photo has a black-and-white effect applied and a dissolve transition is used.

Create Effects with Duplicate Photos

① In the Source list, click an album to make into a slideshow.

② Click a photo that you want to use for the effect.

③ Click **Photos**.

④ Click **Duplicate**.

Note: You can also select a photo and then press ⌘+D to make a duplicate of the photo.

A duplicate of the photo is made within the album.

⑤ Deselect the duplicated photos.

The yellow box disappears from around the photo.

Note: iPhoto makes a slideshow out of the single photo if it is left selected.

⑥ Click .

iPhoto displays a dialog.

⑦ Click .

⑧ Type a name.

⑨ Click **Create**.

iPhoto displays the slideshow in the Source list.

⑩ Click ⬜.

The Slideshow Settings open.

⑪ Click **This Slide**.

⑫ Click the first instance of the duplicate photo in the photo browser.

⑬ Click **Black & White** in the Slideshow Settings.

ON appears at the bottom of the effect, and the slide in the main photo view turns black and white.

⑭ Make sure that the transition you are using for the photo is set to **Dissolve**.

⑮ Click the **Close** button (⬛) to close the Slideshow Settings.

⑯ Click ⬜.

The slideshow plays while showing the effect.

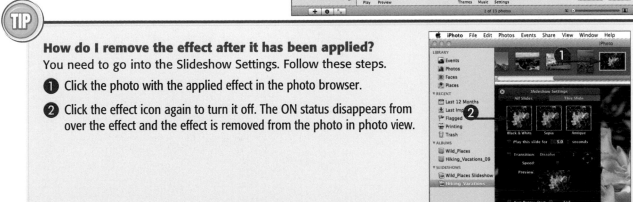

TIP

How do I remove the effect after it has been applied?
You need to go into the Slideshow Settings. Follow these steps.

❶ Click the photo with the applied effect in the photo browser.

❷ Click the effect icon again to turn it off. The ON status disappears from over the effect and the effect is removed from the photo in photo view.

Make Photos into a QuickTime Movie

You can turn a group of photos into a slideshow and play the slideshow using QuickTime Player. Making your photos into a QuickTime movie and burning that movie to CD or DVD enables you to take your slideshows with you and distribute them easily.

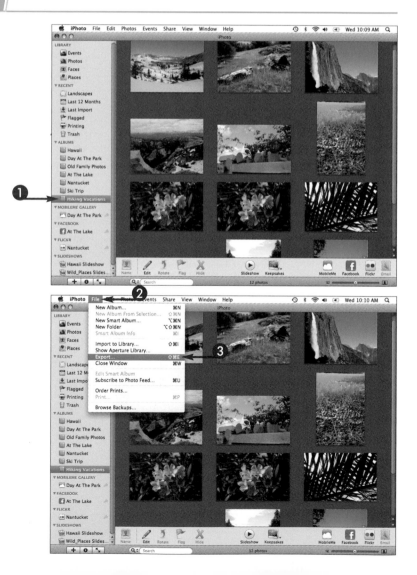

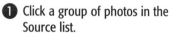

① Click a group of photos in the Source list.

Note: If you do not select a specific event from the Events category, all photos under Events are made into a QuickTime movie.

② Click **File**.

③ Click **Export**.

The Export Photos pane opens.

4 Click **QuickTime**.

Note: Within the Export Photos dialog you can type a new Width and Height for the exported movie. Underneath the Width and Height parameters you can type the duration for each slide.

5 Click **Export**.

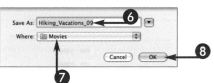

6 Type a name for the movie.

7 Click ⬍ and choose a location on your computer hard drive to save the movie from the pop-up menu.

8 Click **OK**.

The movie is exported to the specified location on the computer hard drive.

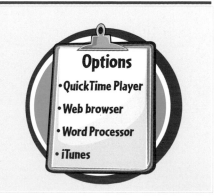

What are my options for playing my newly exported slideshow movie?

The exported slideshow movie of your photos can be played in QuickTime Player or any other application that supports QuickTime, including Web browsers and word processors. You can also import the file into iTunes for playback by using the Add to Library command under the File menu options in the iTunes main menu bar.

Options
- QuickTime Player
- Web browser
- Word Processor
- iTunes

Burn a CD or DVD of Photo Projects

You can create CDs and DVDs to archive your iPhoto photographs by using a process called *burning*.

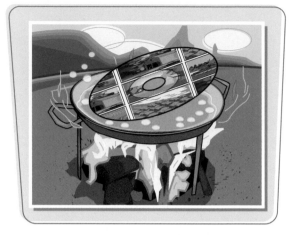

Burn a CD or DVD of Photo Projects

1 In the Source list, select the group of photos that you want to burn to a CD or DVD.

2 Click **Share**.

3 Click **Burn**.

iPhoto prompts you to insert a blank disc to burn photos.

4 Insert a CD-RW disc or blank DVD-R disc into the computer drive and then click **OK**.

Please insert a blank disc to burn photos on a CD or DVD for viewing only in iPhoto.

If you want to create a disc to be viewed on a Windows computer or by a photo processing company, you must use the Burn Disc command in the Finder. For details, visit iPhoto Help.

Burn Disc In: SuperDrive

Cancel   OK

- The iPhoto prompt closes. iPhoto displays a graphical representation of how much disk space will be used during the burn. iPhoto also lists the amount of space used and the available space in megabytes, and lists the number photos being burned to the disk at the bottom of the window.

⑤ Type a new name for the disc being burned, if needed.

⑥ Click **Burn**.

The Burn Disc dialog opens.

⑦ Click **Burn**.

A dialog opens stating that it is burning to the drive. iPhoto will state that the Burn Was Successful in the dialog. If the process was successful, the disk ejects.

Note: When you insert this disk into your computer, it will automatically launch iPhoto to reveal the photos.

 TIP

Can I take a CD that I have burned in iPhoto and play it on a Windows computer?

No. A disk burned in iPhoto cannot be viewed on a computer running a Windows operating system. You can insert the disc in a Mac without iPhoto present or with an older version and view the images in the Finder. The navigation is somewhat awkward, but the images are viewable.

CHAPTER 9

Sharing Photos Online

iPhoto makes it easy for you to share your photography with friends and family on two of the Web's most popular photo-sharing sites, Facebook and Flickr. You can e-mail your photos, export photos to iWeb to build sophisticated Web sites, and publish to online galleries using MobileMe, all within iPhoto. iPhoto also makes it possible to share your photos with other computers across a network.

Prepare Photos for Web Display

If you already have a Web hosting account, iPhoto enables you to save groups of photos as a Web page that can be uploaded to a server for display in a Web browser. Creating a simple Web page is a great way to share your photos with the world.

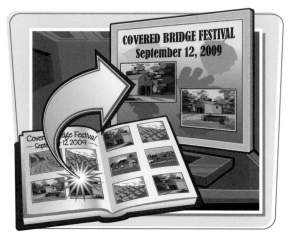

Prepare Photos for Web Display

① Click a collection of photos you want to use on your Web page.

② Click **File**.

③ Click **Export**.

The Export Photos dialog opens.

④ Click the **Web Page** tab.

⑤ Type a title for the Web page.

⑥ Click **Export**.

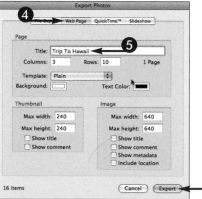

7️⃣ Choose a location to save the Web page.

8️⃣ Click **OK**.

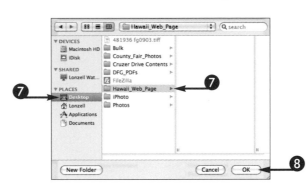

The saved Web page and contents can now be uploaded to a server for display on the Web.

Trip To Hawaii

 TIPS

How can I access characteristics of the page, such as: number of columns, number of rows of pictures, background color, and image height and width?

You can access all of these parameters, and more, from the Web Page pane in Step **4**.

How do I preview the exported Web page to see what it will look like before I publish it to the Web?

Double-click the saved file to open it in a Web browser to preview the Web page.

Publish Albums to a MobileMe Gallery

iPhoto enables you to publish photos directly to your MobileMe Gallery. MobileMe Gallery enables friends and family to actively participate in the sharing of photos by downloading your photos or uploading their own. If you do not have a MobileMe account, click the MobileMe button at the bottom right of the iPhoto interface to learn more.

Publish Albums to a MobileMe Gallery

① Click a collection of photos you want to publish.

② Click the **Plus** button ().

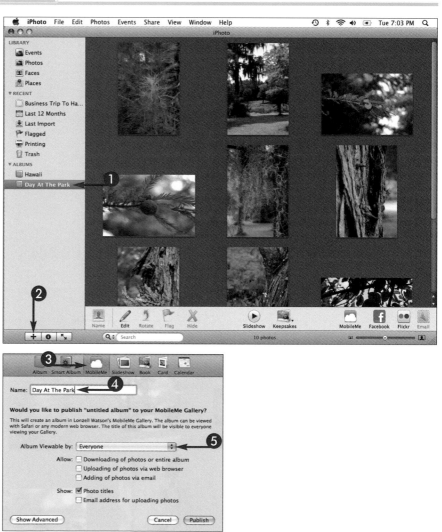

iPhoto displays a dialog.

③ Click the **MobileMe** button (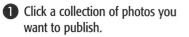).

Note: *If you do not have a MobileMe account, a dialog asks if you want more information.*

④ Type a name for the published album.

⑤ Click ⬦ and select who can view your published photos.

Your Album Viewable by options are: Everyone, Only me, or Edit Names and Passwords, which lets you specify passwords or limit viewing to certain groups or individuals.

6 Click to choose publishing options in the **Allow** and **Show** categories (☐ changes to ☑).

Note: You can click the Show Advanced button for more publishing options.

7 Click **Publish**.

iPhoto publishes the photo album.

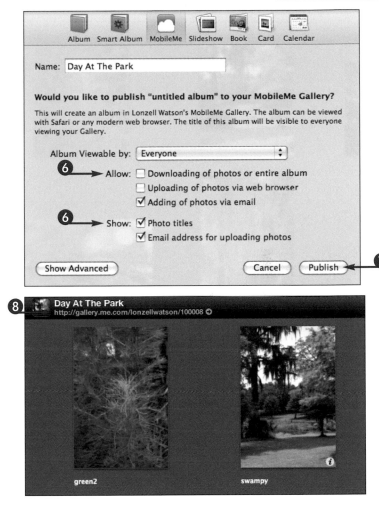

The contents of the album appear in the viewing area along with a Web site address below the title.

8 Click the address to view the Web site.

Is there a quick way to let people know that I have posted a photo album?
Yes. Click the **Tell a Friend** button (🖼) to send an announcement e-mail to friends and family about your published album. iPhoto sends a URL to the gallery in an e-mail, along with a password for the album, if you opted to use a password.

Can I upload photos directly from my phone?
Yes. The e-mail address of the published album appears in the header of the viewing area. You can use the address to e-mail photos from your iPhone.

Subscribe to Published Photo Albums

You can share photos with friends and family by subscribing to each other's MobileMe photo albums. iPhoto makes it easy to see new photos as your friends and family update their albums.

Note: *You will need the Web address of a published album to follow these steps.*

① Use a Web browser to go to the published Web album address.

② Click the **Subscribe** button () to open the Subscribe dialog.

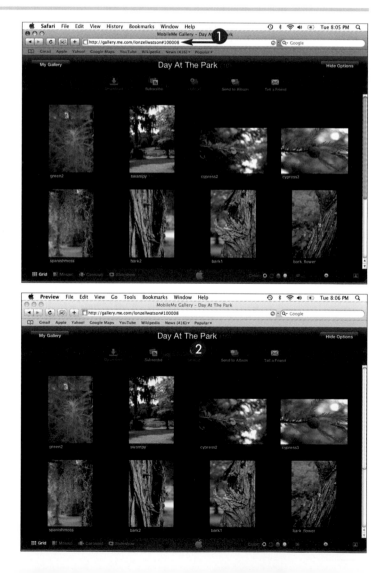

3 Click the **in iPhoto** option
(○ changes to ◉).

The album appears in your iPhoto
Source list.

Note: *Click RSS to view the photo album in your
favorite RSS reader.*

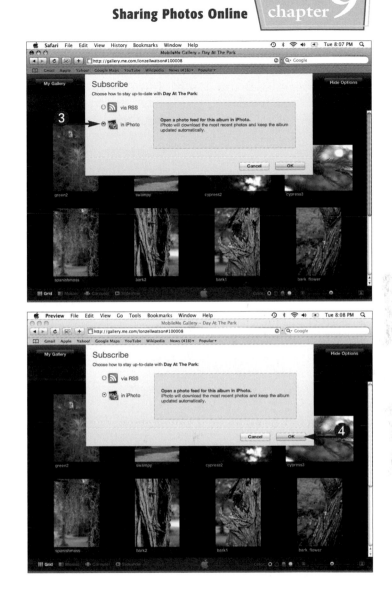

4 Click **OK**.

You can now view the published
photo album.

**How do I check for updates to the published album to which I
have subscribed?**

iPhoto automatically updates the subscribed album in the Source list.
You can specify how often iPhoto checks for new updates by going to
iPhoto in the main menu bar and clicking Preferences. Follow these
steps:

1 Click the **Web** button ().

2 Choose an automatic time frame.

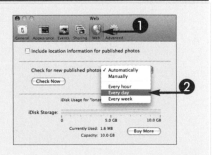

Export Photos to iWeb

iWeb enables you to design and publish your own Web site. You can export a group of photos from iPhoto directly to a Web page designed for displaying images in iPhoto. Using iWeb to publish your photos gives you more options when it comes to the designing of Web pages and can allow you to add your own personal touch to Web pages.

Note: You need a Web hosting service in order to publish a Web site.

1 Choose a group of photos that you want to export.

2 Click **Share** in the main menu.

3 Click **Send to iWeb**.

4 Click **Photo Page**.

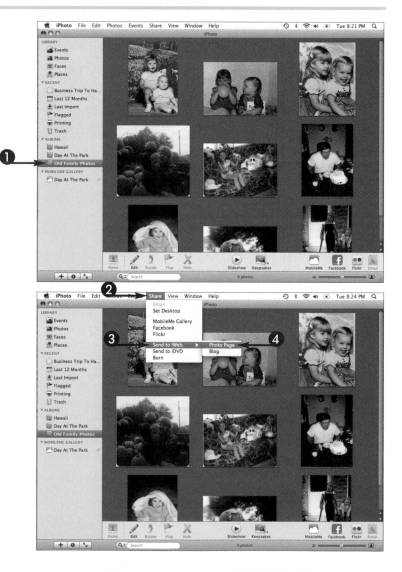

The iWeb application opens.

5 Click the template you want to use.

6 Click **Choose**.

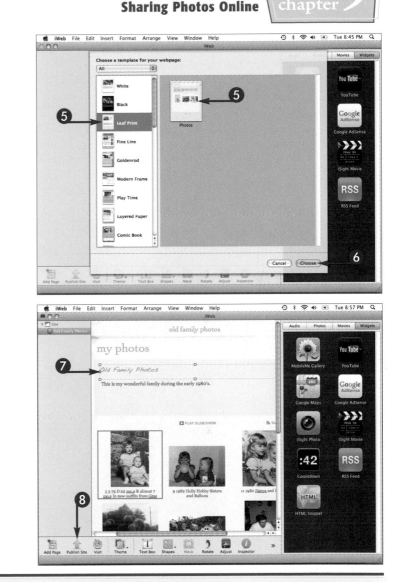

iWeb displays the group of photos that you chose in iPhoto in the specified template.

7 Edit the iWeb template.

You can personalize the text in the template and much more.

8 Click the **Publish Site** button () to publish to your MobileMe account.

If you do not have a MobileMe account, you can publish to a folder in iWeb, then upload that folder to your Web hosting account with an FTP client.

TIPS

Do I need a MobileMe account to publish a Web site?

No. You can maintain a Web site using another Web hosting service, if you have a local Web server, or if your computer has Web Sharing turned on under the Mac OS X System Preferences.

Some of my photos are very large files. Will this cause slow loading of Web pages?

iPhoto automatically reduces the scale of large photos so that Web pages are more easily loaded and displayed.

Publish Photos to Facebook

You can publish photos to your Facebook account so that your Facebook friends can view your images.

① Choose a group of photos that you want to publish.

② Click the **Facebook** button ().

A set up iPhoto to publish dialog opens and asks if you want to set up iPhoto to publish to Facebook.

③ Click **Set Up** if you are not logged in to Facebook, or if you want to sign up for Facebook.

④ Type your user name and password.

Note: *You can click the **Sign up for Facebook** link and follow the site's instructions to create an account.*

⑤ Click **Login** in the Facebook dialog.

⑥ Click **Close**.

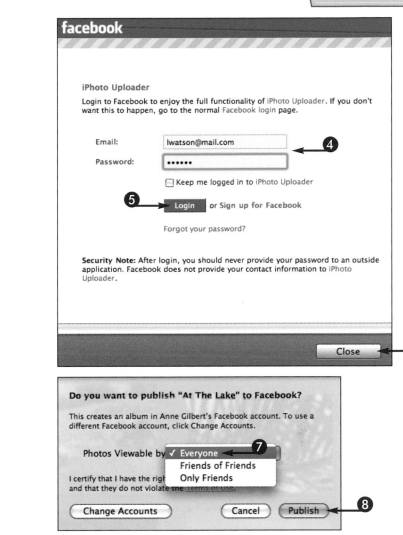

The dialog closes and a publishing to Facebook dialog appears.

⑦ Choose an option in the **Photos Viewable by** pop-up menu.

⑧ Click **Publish**.

The photos appear in the Source list as a published album.

You can view the photos that you have just published to Facebook by clicking the Web site address at the top of the viewing window.

Note: *You can delete the album in the Source list to remove the photos from the Web site.*

How do I add photos to a published album?
You can move photos into the album while on the Facebook site. You can also add photos to the published album from within iPhoto. Follow these steps to add photos to a published album from within iPhoto:

① Select the photos that you want to add to Facebook.

② Drag the photos to the published album in the Source list.

You can share photo albums online by publishing to your Flickr account.

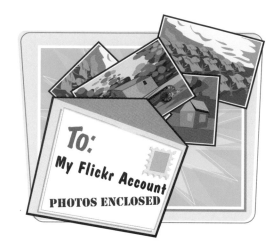

Share Photos on Flickr

① Choose a group of photos that you want to publish.

② Click the **Flickr** button ().

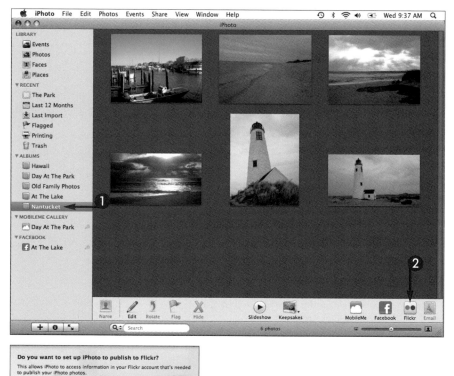

A dialog opens and asks if you want to set up iPhoto to publish to Flickr.

③ Click **Set Up** if you are not logged into Flickr or want to sign up for a Flickr account.

The Flickr Web site opens where you can choose to **Sign Up** for an account or **Sign In** if you already have an account.

④ Type your Yahoo Password in the Flickr Web page.

⑤ Click **Sign In.**

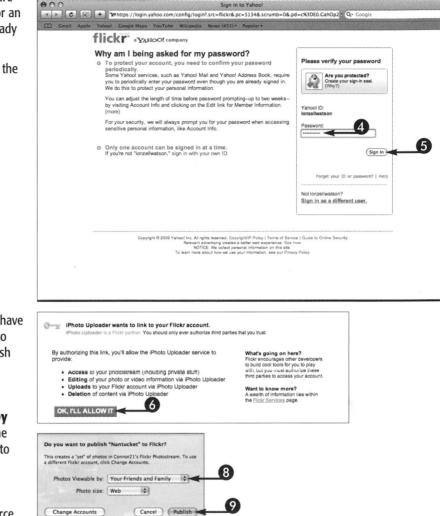

⑥ Click **OK, I'll Allow It** if you have not already authorized Flickr to use its uploading tool to publish photos.

⑦ Close the Web site window.

⑧ Click the **Photos Viewable by** ◆ to specify who can view the photos and designate the photo size from the pop-up menu.

⑨ Click **Publish.**

The photos appear in the Source list as a published album.

Note: *You can delete the album in the Source list to remove the photos from the Web site.*

How do I add photos to a published album?
You can move photos into the album, which is referred to as a set, while on the Flickr site. You can also add photos to the published album from within iPhoto by dragging the photos to the published album in the Source list.

If you have a photo that you want to share with
a friend or family member, and you know his or
her e-mail address, you can send the image in an
e-mail.

① Click the photo you want to send.

② Click **Share** in the main menu.

③ Click **Email**.

*Note: You can also click the **Email** button (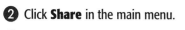).*

The Mail Photo dialog appears.

④ Click the **Size** ⬍, and then choose the size you want to use for the sent photo from the pop-up menu.

⑤ Click **Compose Message.**

iPhoto creates a new mail message in your default mail client.

The photo appears in the message body.

Note: *Out of the gate, iPhoto supports Apple Mail, Eudora, Entourage, and AOL. A freeware utility named iPhoto MailerPatcher allows you to extend to other mail clients.*

⑥ Type the address of the recipient into the **To** field.

⑦ Type a subject in the **Subject** field.

⑧ Click **Send**.

Apple Mail sends the message.

How do I insert text above the photo in the e-mail?
Adding text to the body of the letter enables you to introduce the photo so that the recipient knows why you are sending it. Follow theses steps to add text:

① Click in the left area of the photograph in the e-mail.

② Press Return on the keyboard.

③ Press ⬆ on the keyboard.

The cursor moves to the new line above the photograph.

④ Type the message.

Share Photos Across a Network

If your computer is connected to other computers across a local area network, you can share photo albums, slideshows, books, calendars, and cards with up to five other computers. Sharing photos across a network is a convenient way to share your photos with others.

Note: *You can share photos with up to five other computers in the same subnet as your computer. Check under Network located in the Internet & Network pane of the Mac OS X System Preferences to see which subnet your computer is in.*

① Click **iPhoto** in the main menu.

② Click **Preferences**.

③ Click **Sharing**.

④ Click the **Share my photos** check box (☐ changes to ☑).

⑤ Choose which photos to share.

You can choose to **Share entire library** (⦿) or **Share selected albums** (☑) and specify selected photo collections.

6 Type a name for the shared photo items.

Note: The name that you supply here is what shows up in the Source list on other computers configured to look for shared photos on the network.

7 Click **Require password**
(changes to ☑) if you want access to the photos on your computer password protected.

8 Type a password if you have chosen to make your photo items password protected.

9 Close the sharing dialog.

10 Leave iPhoto open on your computer for others to access your shared items across a network.

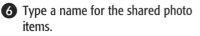

How do I find other shared photos on my network?

As long as the Look for shared photos option is checked in the Sharing pane, iPhoto automatically looks for shared iPhoto content across the network. When it finds photos that are shared, the name for the shared collection of photos appears in the Source list.

Are shared photos only viewable?

No, you can view and also import shared photos that are streamed over the network.

Making Prints and Exporting Photos

iPhoto's printing and export options provide an easy and intuitive outlet for photographers to produce professional-quality prints and to create Web pages. You can choose to make your own prints, choosing from standard print sizes, creating contact sheets, and adding borders and mats to your photos. iPhoto also provides you easy access to order your own professionally made prints, as well as create high-quality photo DVDs using iDVD.

The iPhoto print options and tools enable you to produce high-quality prints. Knowing how photo resolution, types of printing paper, and the iPhoto print options each play an important role in the quality of your prints helps you make good printing decisions.

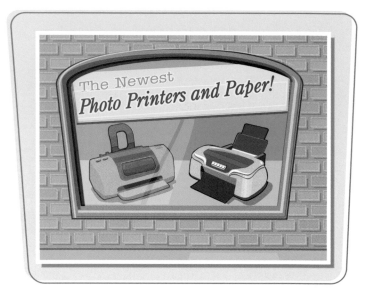

Photo Resolution

The resolution of a photo refers to the number of pixels per inch in the image. The higher the resolution of a photograph, the sharper and more detailed the picture, up to a point. Once the resolution exceeds that of the output device, you can have problems with bleed and moiré. The advantage of choosing a higher-resolution camera is that you have more pixels to work with, which results in a larger image. A larger image means there is less need for magnification, which degrades the image, to produce prints of a larger size.

Types of Printers

If your goal is to produce photo-realistic prints, investing in a printer specifically designed for photo printing yields the best results. Photo printers such as the Epson Stylus Photo series, HP Photosmart, and the Canon PIXMA series are thoroughly the same price as standard inkjet printers, but due to the quantity and type of ink cartridges they use, can prove much more expensive. With that being said, these photo printers can produce beautiful, photo-realistic prints.

Printing Paper

The quality of paper that you use is very important with regards to the image quality that your photo printer is able to reproduce. Be sure to use photo papers with your photo printer because they result in sharper and more vivid prints than the standard, thin copy paper. Photo paper is much more expensive than plain paper but the high-quality end result is very evident.

Printer Settings

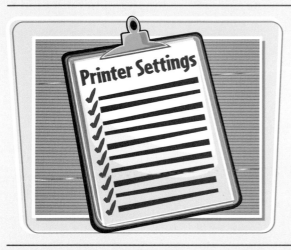

Make sure that your printer settings are properly configured before you actually print. Most printers can accept various qualities and sizes of paper, and print in different sizes as well. Printing with the wrong printer settings can result in a lot of wasted ink and paper.

Ordering Prints

If you do not have a high-quality photo printer, iPhoto makes it easy for you to order professional prints online. You can order wallet-size photos and up to 20-x-30-inch posters using the Kodak Print Service. To make an order, you first need to create an Apple account.

Print Photos

iPhoto gives you many options for printing your own photos. You can choose from options that include printing full page (with or without borders), in standard and customized sizes, as well as printing contact sheets, or with a mat.

1 Select a photo that you want to print.

Note: You can also select a group of photos to print.

2 Click **File** in the main menu bar.

3 Click **Print**.

The photo or photos that you selected appear in the Print Setting view.

4 Choose a theme from the left side of the menu.

The preview area shows how your photo or photos look in the selected theme.

*Note: You can click **Customize** to further customize your print job.*

5 Click 🔼 and choose the correct printer.

6 Click 🔼 and choose the type of paper on which you want to print.

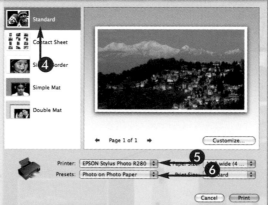

7 Click ▣ and choose the paper size.

The preview area shows how your photo or photos look on the selected paper size.

8 Click ▣ and choose the print size.

The preview area shows how your photo or photos look in the selected print size.

9 Click **Print**.

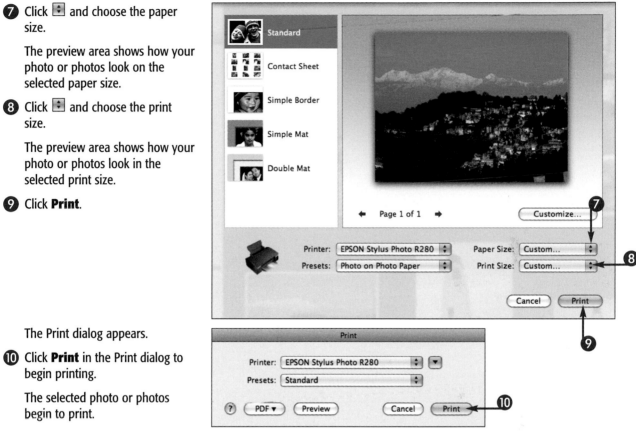

The Print dialog appears.

10 Click **Print** in the Print dialog to begin printing.

The selected photo or photos begin to print.

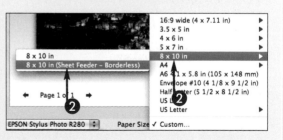

TIP

Can I make a print that does not have a border?

Yes. A print that has no border, where the image extends to the edges of the paper, is commonly referred to as *full bleed*. If your printer supports full-bleed printing, you can easily print an image that has no white space around it. Follow these steps:

1 Follow Steps **1** to **7** in the steps.

2 Choose a paper size and then choose the Borderless option at the bottom of the menu.

3 Follow Steps **8** to **10** to print the image.

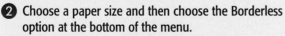

Explore Customize Print Options

You can click the Customize button in the Print Settings dialog and adjust settings including background color and layout, and add captions to printed photographs. iPhoto also enables you to make edits to photos just for a specific print job, without affecting every representation of the photo in the Library. You can conveniently make adjustments to exposure, highlights, and shadows, and even add effects for the print job only.

● **Themes**

You can change the theme of your print and see what it will look like in the preview area. Your choices for themes are Standard, Contact Sheet, Simple Border, Simple Mat, and Double Mat.

● **Background**

You can choose the background color of a border for your printed image by choosing the Background category. Your choices are white, gray, and black. If you do not see a preview with a border, click the Borders button (🔲) and choose an option with a border, and then choose a background.

● **Borders**

You can choose a style for the border that will surround your printed photograph. By default, this option is set to 1, which is without a border. Choose another option to see the choices you make in the Background category.

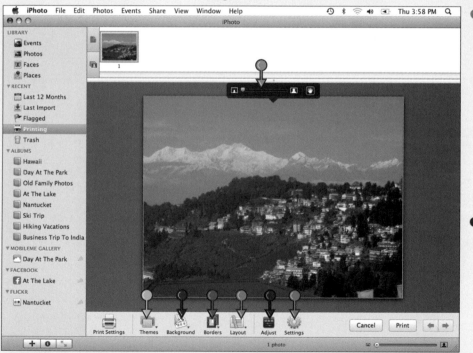

● **Layout**

You can choose how many instances of a photograph are placed on a single print, and select layout options with captions. The option to print multiple instances of a single image is not available for the Standard or Contact Sheet themes.

● **Adjust**

You can manipulate settings such as Exposure, Contrast, Highlights and Shadows, as well as add effects by using the Adjust button (🔲). When you use the Adjust button, the edits are made for the print job only. If 🔲 is dimmed, click the image in the preview area to activate it.

● **Settings**

You can choose the font type and size of the captions by accessing the Settings option. iPhoto enables you to specify one photo per page, show crop marks, or autoflow pages.

● **Editing Tools**

You can crop and reframe a photo using editing tools, for a print project only. The photo has to be selected for the editing tools to appear. This limited cropping ability allows you to easily make last-second changes to produce the perfect print.

iPhoto enables you to export images for use in other programs by changing their file size and changing their format. You can export Web pages, export photos as a QuickTime movie, as well as optimize photos for other electronic devices such as an iPod. The iPhoto Export dialog offers a variety of export possibilities to suit your needs.

● **Exporting Files for Use in Other Programs**

You can use the File Export pane in the Export dialog to choose a different file format for files that may be used in other programs. You can specify picture size for images that you may want to make smaller for faster download speeds on the Web or to send as an attachment in an e-mail. You also have the ability to export groups of photos in a sequence, or determine whether they are listed by file name, album name, or iPhoto titles.

● **Export Web Pages**

You can export a group of photos as a Web page that you can then upload to a Web server to share with friends and family. iPhoto gives you the flexibility of determining how the page will look by letting you specify the number of columns and rows per page, the dimensions of the thumbnails, and how the photo descriptions appear. Under Share in the iPhoto main menu bar, you also have the option of sharing your photos online using MobileMe, Facebook, Flickr, and iWeb.

● **Export a QuickTime Movie**

You can export a QuickTime movie of your photos that can be played using QuickTime player, or Web browsers and word processors that support QuickTime. iPhoto enables you to specify the dimensions of the movie, add background colors, and make decisions concerning the music played in the movie.

● **Export Slideshow to Electronic Devices**

You can optimize your slideshows for play on popular electronic devices such as an iPod, iPhone, Apple TV, and your computer. You can also optimize your slideshow for iTunes and for use with your MobileMe account.

Export Photos

| File Export | Web Page | QuickTime™ | Slideshow |

Kind: JPEG

JPEG Quality: Medium

Include: ☐ Title and keywords
☐ Location information

Size: Full Size

File Name: Use filename

Prefix for sequential:

11 items

Cancel | Export

Crop a Photo in a Print Project

You can crop a photo just for the current print project. The cropping performed is not reflected in all representations of the photo in the iPhoto Library. iPhoto gives you the flexibility to make last-second editing decisions so you can print the perfect picture.

Crop a Photo in a Print Project

1 Choose the photograph that you want to print.

2 Click **File** in the main menu bar.

3 Click **Print**.

The Print Settings dialog opens.

4 Click **Customize**.

The photo project opens in Print Project view and the print project icon appears in the Source list.

5 Select the photo.

The Edit tools appear.

6 Drag the size slider 🔘 to the right.

The image magnifies and the Hand tool is activated.

7 Click and drag around in the picture with the Hand tool to reframe the image.

8 Click **Print**.

9 In the Print dialog, click **Print** to begin printing.

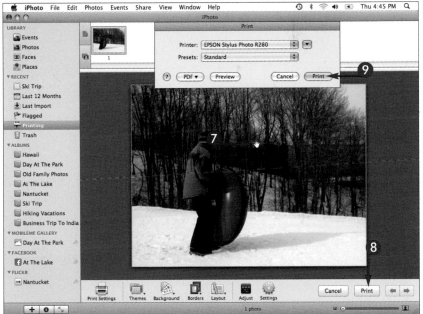

Why does my print look fuzzy after cropping?

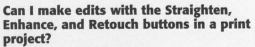

It is possible that the image was taken at a low resolution and you cropped the image too much, and did not retain enough pixels for a high-quality print. If you cut off too much of a low-resolution photo, the pixels have to be stretched to fit a larger print area, and therefore, the image will be fuzzy. Try not cropping the image so much.

Can I make edits with the Straighten, Enhance, and Retouch buttons in a print project?

Yes. You can use the iPhoto basic edit tools on photos in a print project. Control -click the photo in Print Project view a **Photo** from the menu. Any edits Edit view will be reflected in all representations of the photo in the iPhoto Library.

Remove Photo
Fit Photo to Frame Size
Mirror Image

Move to Front
Send to Back

Edit Photo ◄────────

Print a Photo Multiple Times on a Page

If you have a photo that you want to print and distribute to friends and family, iPhoto enables you to print a single image multiple times on a page. You can save paper and time by printing a single image multiple times on a single sheet of paper and then cutting the copies out.

Print a Photo Multiple Times on a Page

① Select the photo that you want to print.

② Click **File** in the main menu bar.

③ Click **Print**.

The Print Settings dialog appears.

④ Click ⬍ and choose a paper size.

Note: Letter or Legal size works well for multiple images.

The photo can now be seen on the specified paper in the preview area.

⑤ Click ⬍ and choose a print size.

The photo is adjusted to match the specified print size in the preview dialog.

⑥ Click **Customize**.

The photo project opens in Print Project view and the print project icon appears in the Source list.

7 Click the **Settings** button (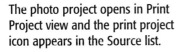).

8 In the Settings dialog, click the **Photos Per Page** .

9 Choose **Multiple of the same photo per page** from the pop-up menu.

10 Click **OK**.

Multiple instances of the photo appear on the page in the preview window.

11 Click **Print**.

The Print dialog opens.

12 Click **Print** in the Print dialog to begin printing.

 TIPS

How can I undo the zoom and cropping that iPhoto performs after I choose to place multiple instances of the same photo on a page?

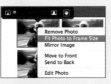

To undo the zoom and crop that occur, Control-click each image and choose **Fit Photo to Frame Size** from the menu.

Can I print on perforated paper in iPhoto?

Yes. If your printer supports perforated paper, the option appears under the Paper Size options in the Print Settings dialog. If you do not see a perforated option under Paper Size, your printer does not support it or you may not have installed the correct driver. Refer to your printer's manual.

Print a Contact Sheet

You can create and print a contact sheet in iPhoto with just a few clicks. iPhoto makes it easy for you to print a collection of photos on a single sheet for easy reference.

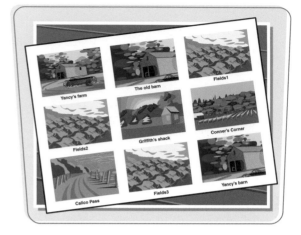

① Select a group of photos to print.

An Event is selected in the example.

② Click **File** in the main menu bar.

③ Click **Print**.

The Print Settings dialog appears.

④ Click **Contact Sheet** in the Themes menu.

The display area shows what the photos will look like when printed.

⑤ Click **Customize** to change the number of columns in which the photos appear.

- The photo project opens in Print Edit view, and the Print Project icon (🖶 Printing) appears in the Source list.

6 Drag the Columns slider right to increase the number of columns or left to decrease the number of columns.

The changes made to the number of columns are reflected in the preview area.

7 Click **Print**.

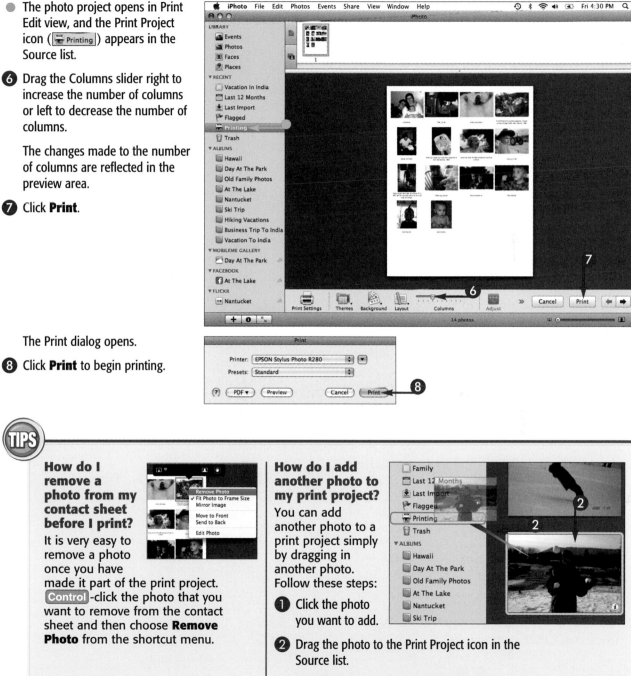

The Print dialog opens.

8 Click **Print** to begin printing.

How do I remove a photo from my contact sheet before I print?

It is very easy to remove a photo once you have made it part of the print project. Control-click the photo that you want to remove from the contact sheet and then choose **Remove Photo** from the shortcut menu.

How do I add another photo to my print project?

You can add another photo to a print project simply by dragging in another photo. Follow these steps:

1 Click the photo you want to add.

2 Drag the photo to the Print Project icon in the Source list.

The photo is added to the print project.

Order Professional Prints

You can order professional-quality prints of your photos within iPhoto after setting up a 1-click account. The iPhoto print service makes it easy for you to choose print sizes and quantity, and designate a shipping address for your professional prints.

Note: *You must crop all of the photos for which you want to order professional prints to match the aspect ratio you want to print, such as 4 x 6, or 5 x 7, before beginning the following steps.*

1 Select the group of cropped photos in the Source list for which you want to have professional prints.

2 Click **File**.

3 Click **Order Prints**.

The Order Prints dialog opens containing the selected photos.

Note: *If this is your first time placing an order, you will be prompted to set up an account. You can click Set Up Account and follow the instructions to set up an account.*

4 Click the size of the photo you want to have printed.

● If you want 4-x-6-inch prints, you can click the **Quick Order** arrows to specify the number of sets you want to order of each photo.

5 Type the number of photos you want to have printed.

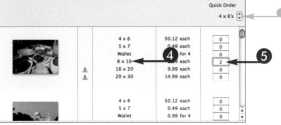

⑥ Click the **Ship To** 🔽 and choose a shipping address from the pop-up menu.

⑦ Click the **Ship Via** 🔽 and choose the method of shipping from the pop-up menu.

Ship To:	Myself	⑥	Subtotal:	$16.91
Ship Via:	Standard ($2.99)	⑦	Tax (Estimated):	1.10
			Shipping:	2.99

Usually ships in 1–3 business days.

Sizes and availability are based on your United States billing address. Pricing is in US Dollars.

⚠ Low resolution may result in poor print quality.

Order Total: **$21.00**

(?) (Account Info) (Cancel) (Buy Now)

Note: You should review the entire order to confirm the order and total before proceeding.

⑧ Click **Buy Now** to place the order.

Note: You can check the status of your order at www.apple.com/support/photoservices/ww/.

Ship To:	Myself		Subtotal:	$16.91
Ship Via:	Standard ($2.99)		Tax (Estimated):	1.10
			Shipping:	2.99

Usually ships in 1–3 business days.

Sizes and availability are based on your United States billing address. Pricing is in US Dollars.

⚠ Low resolution may result in poor print quality.

Order Total: **$21.00**

(?) (Account Info) (Cancel) (Buy Now)

⑧

TIPS

How do I edit my shipping address?

To edit the shipping address, you must click the **Account Info** button in the bottom right of the Order Prints dialog. You have to enter your Apple ID and password and then click **Sign In**. The Account Info dialog opens and you have access to edit your Apple ID, billing, and shipping information. You also have the chance to read the Terms and Conditions as well as the Privacy Policy.

What does the yellow alert markers mean in the Order Prints dialog?

The yellow markers are low-resolution alerts and appear next to print sizes that are not optimal for a particular photo's resolution. Choose a smaller print size for the clearest print.

Create a Photo DVD in iDVD

You can send your photos from iPhoto to iDVD to design a high-quality DVD. iPhoto also enables you to transfer movies taken with your DSLR or point-and-shoot camera to iDVD. Sending your projects to iDVD allows you to showcase your photos on a television set in a sleek DVD presentation.

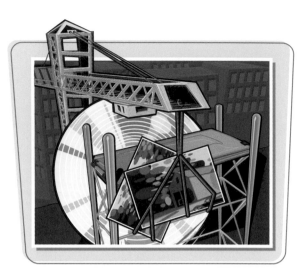

Note: You will need a blank DVD inserted into your computer for this task.

① Select the group of photos in the Source list that you want to send to iDVD.

② Click **Share**.

③ Click **Send to iDVD**.

iDVD opens and the photos are placed into an iDVD template.

A slideshow button is automatically created in the DVD menu with the name of the group of photos sent from iPhoto.

④ Choose an iDVD theme.

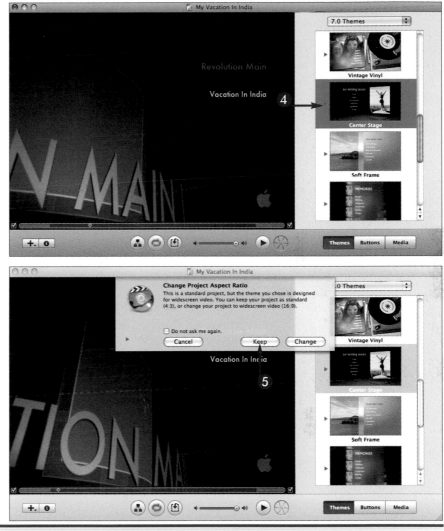

A dialog appears, asking if you want to change the project aspect ratio from standard to widescreen.

⑤ Click **Keep** if you will be viewing the disk in 4:3 standard format; click **Change** if you will be viewing it in 16:9 widescreen format on your television.

The option to Keep the project as standard 4:3 was chosen in this example.

TIP

Can I preview the DVD before I burn the disk?

Yes, you can run a simulation of your DVD before burning it by following these steps:

① Click the **Preview DVD** button (▶) located next to the Burn button.

② Click the **enter** button in the remote control to play the simulation.

continued

You can personalize the menu of your DVD by adding pictures and music. iDVD also lets you customize your slideshow by letting you specify slide duration, transition type, and more. You can also rearrange the slides in the slideshow.

The template opens.

⑥ Double-click the text in the iDVD theme to edit it.

As you begin to edit the text, the options for font type, typeface, and button size appear.

⑦ Click **Media**.

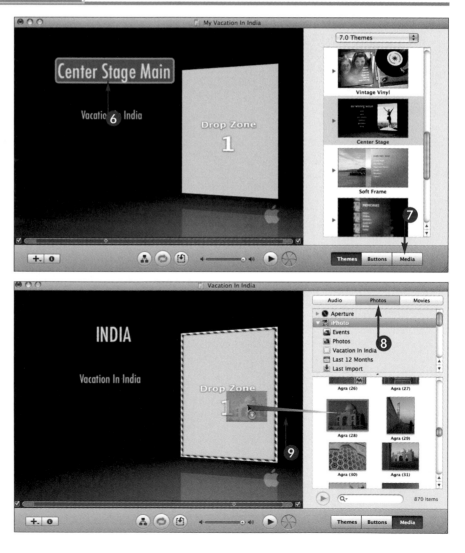

You can now browse for audio, photos, and movies on your computer hard drive.

⑧ Click **Photos**.

The photos within the iPhoto Library appear.

⑨ Drag a photo from the media browser that you want to use in the DVD menu, and drop it in Drop Zone 1 in the iDVD main viewing area.

The photo now appears on the DVD's menu.

⑩ Click **Audio**.

⑪ Click **iTunes**.

The iTunes Music Library appears.

⑫ Click and drag the song you want to use for the DVD menu and drop it on the menu.

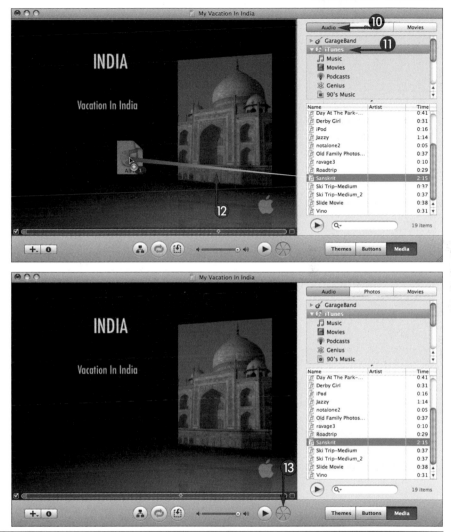

The new music plays.

⑬ Click the **Burn** button to burn the DVD project to a disc.

The burning process begins.

TIP

How do I customize the various slideshow settings, such as slideshow duration and transitions?

You can make adjustments to your slideshow in iDVD by double-clicking the button for the slideshow in your DVD menu. Within the slideshow editor you can change the order of images in a slideshow, specify slide duration, and much more.

Convert File Format and Change Photo Dimensions upon Export

You can use the File Export option in the iPhoto Export dialog to prepare images for use in other applications. You can specify the dimensions of images to optimize them for faster download on the Web, or to send as an e-mail attachment. iPhoto also enables you to change the file format of the image for your convenience.

Convert File Format and Change Photo Dimensions upon Export

① Select the file or files that you want to export.

② Click **File**.

③ Click **Export**.

The Export Photos dialog appears.

④ Click **File Export**.

⑤ Click the **Kind** ⬆ and choose the format in which you want to save the file from the pop-up menu.

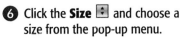
6 Click the **Size** ⬍ and choose a size from the pop-up menu.

7 Click **Export**.

Export Photos

File Export | Web Page | QuickTime™ | Slideshow

Kind: TIFF

JPEG Quality: Medium

Include: ☐ Title and keywords
☐ Location information

Size: Small ◄ **6**

File Name: Use filename

Prefix for sequential:

3 items   (Cancel) (Export ◄ **7**)

The Export dialog appears.

8 Click a location to save the files.

9 Click **OK**.

The files export to the specified location.

◄ ► | 88 ≣ ▥ | 📁 Exported Pics ⬍ | Q search

▼ DEVICES **8**
  🖥 Macintosh HD
  💽 iDisk

▼ SHARED
  🖥 Lonzell Wat...

▼ PLACES
  🖥 Desktop
  🏠 Lonzell
  📂 Applications
  📄 Documents

📁 100% ▶
📁 Exported Pics ▶
🗎 FileZilla
📁 Travel Destinations ▶
🗎 Vacation In India.dvdproj
📁 Vacation_Plans ▶

(New Folder)   (Cancel) (OK ◄ **9**)

Can I export a RAW file that has been edited and therefore saved by iPhoto as a JPEG?

Yes. If you imported a RAW file into iPhoto and then edited that RAW file, iPhoto saves that file as a JPEG. In order to export that file the way it was originally brought into iPhoto, as a RAW file, you must choose the **Original** option from the Kind field in the Export dialog.

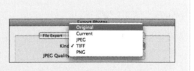

Export a Slideshow to an iPod

You can optimize your slideshows for play on an iPod or iPhone by using the Slideshow export options. iPhoto exports your slideshow to fit the display size of the device so all you have to do is sync it to the device using iTunes. iPhoto makes it easy for you to take your slideshows with you on the road through your iPod or iPhone.

Export a Slideshow to an iPod

1 Select the group of photos that you want to export as a slideshow.

2 Click **File** in the main menu bar.

3 Click **Export**.

The Export Photos dialog appears.

4 Click **Slideshow**.

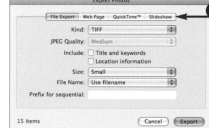

The Slideshow options appear.

5 Click **Medium** to optimize the slideshow for iPod viewing.

Note: It is important that you leave Automatically send slideshow to iTunes checked so you can immediately connect the iPod and begin syncing.

6 Click **Export**.

iPhoto lets you pick a location to save the file.

7 Click ⬍ and choose a location to save the file.

8 Click **OK**.

The slideshow is exported to the specified location.

iTunes automatically opens after the export so you can view the slideshow or sync it to an iPod.

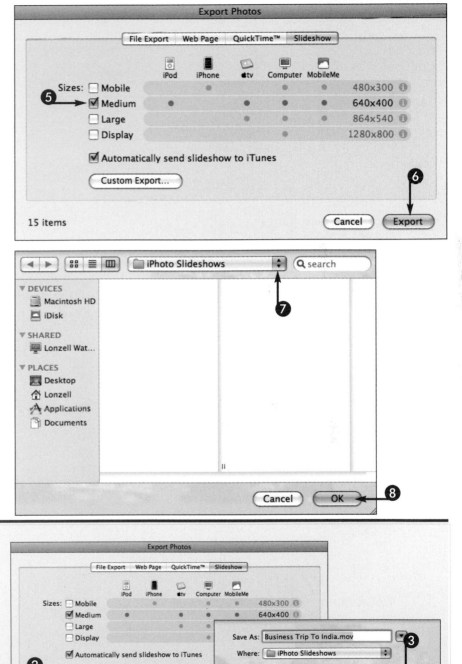

TIP

Can I customize my settings for my exported slideshow?

Yes. You can customize export movie settings.

1 Follow Steps **1** to **4** in this task to open the Slideshow export options.

2 Click **Custom Export**.

3 Click **Options** to access the Movie Settings dialog.

CHAPTER

11

Creating Photo Books

iPhoto's book, calendar, and card themes were made to streamline the process of creating high-quality keepsakes, easily. You can choose to have iPhoto lay out the project for you, lay out your projects manually, or perform a combination of both. iPhoto offers a variety of project sizes and designs from which to choose, and photos can be easily swapped, added, and edited within projects. After you complete your project, you can order professional prints and have them delivered to your door.

Plan a Photo Book

iPhoto enables you to design and order professionally bound photo books that can be shipped to your home, or to a friend or relative as a gift. Understanding the process of creating a photo book in iPhoto allows you to plan your project in advance and produce a higher-quality book in a shorter amount of time.

Choose Photos

The book type and theme play a large role in the size and quantity of photos you will use on each book page. Browsing the iPhoto themes and creating an album of the photos you want to use before you begin the project helps you form the story you want to tell in the book. Organizing your photos before you begin also helps you to choose photographs that complement each other on a two-page spread. Consider shooting your photos for a specific iPhoto theme.

Prepare Photos

If your camera does not capture images in the 4x3 aspect ratio, the same aspect ratio that iPhoto displays photos, your photos may not align properly when presented side by side in a book. This also goes for photographs that you may have cropped, but did not constrain the aspect ratio to the 4x3 ratio. To prevent this alignment issue in your book, use iPhoto to crop the photos to a 4x3 size ratio before you begin a project.

Choose a Book Type (Size)

The book size that you choose is largely dictated by your budget and the overall design that you want to achieve. Large or Medium-size Softcover are less expensive choices than Large Hardcover, but Large Hardcover gives you the most design flexibility. You also need to consider the resolution of your photos. Choose smaller book sizes for lower-resolution photos for best results.

Select a Theme

Each book theme provides you a variety of color schemes and arrangements to present your photographs. Not all themes support text, so if you want to include short descriptions or thoughts, choose a theme that can support the amount of text you want to use. The Picture Book theme can support up to 16 images per page with no text, and Folio can support only 2, but with caption space.

Autoflow or Manual

You can let iPhoto place the images on the pages in your photo book by choosing the Autoflow option, or you can simply drag and drop the images on the pages manually. The drawback of letting iPhoto place the images itself is that you may not always agree with the photo arrangement. If you choose Autoflow, you can still arrange photos manually.

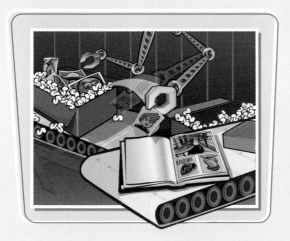

Order the Book

After you finish your masterpiece, you can click **Buy Book** to order it online. Before you can order, you first need to sign up for an Apple account. After you have an account, you can specify a quantity, recipient, shipping method, and a cover color (if you have created a hardcover book).

Create a Photo Book

iPhoto provides a variety of book sizes and designs to create your own professional photo books. You can streamline the process even further and let iPhoto place the photos on individual book pages by choosing Autoflow, or you can place them manually.

Create a Photo Book

1 Select a group of photos that you want to use in the book.

2 Click the **Book** button (🖼).

● Based on the resolution of your screen, or when the iPhoto window is less than 1024 pixels in width, you may need to click **Keepsakes** (🖼) and then click the **Book** button (🖼) as seen in this example.

The book dialog appears.

3 Click the **Book Type** ⬍ and choose the size option from the pop-up menu.

4 Select a book theme.

The Travel Book theme is depicted in the preview area of the dialog.

5 Click **Choose**.

● iPhoto switches to Book view and the new book appears in the Source list.

A dialog opens to inform you that you can either drag your photos onto the pages or choose Autoflow to lay out the book automatically.

⑥ Click **OK**.

A blank cover page is in the main viewing area.

Note: *At this point you could click the Autoflow button at the bottom of the interface to have iPhoto insert all the photos into pages automatically.*

Note: *Keep in mind that Autoflow uses every image you have designated for use in the book.*

⑦ Drag photos from the photo browser located at the top of the interface and drop them one at a time into each empty gray area on the cover.

The photos now appear on the cover page.

Note: *Thumbnails in the photo browser display a small check mark to indicate that they have been used in the book. You can still reuse the photos.*

⑧ Click in each text field below and type a new title and subtitle.

⑨ Click the **Page View** button () to the left of the photo browser.

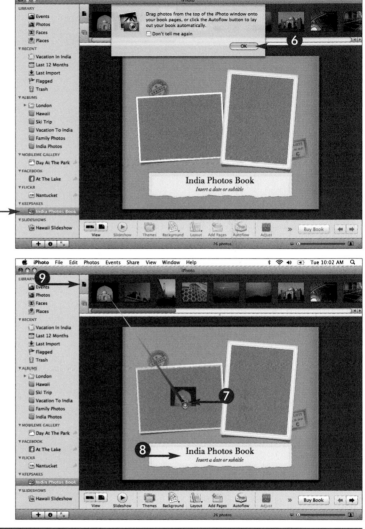

TIP

Can I enlarge or crop a photo I have placed in a book?

Yes, you can enlarge and crop an image to adjust the framing of the subject matter in the photo. Follow these steps.

① Click the photo once to make the zoom slider appear.

② Move the slider to the right to enlarge the photo.

③ Use the Hand tool to reframe the photo.

iPhoto enables you to personalize your photo books by adding descriptions and changing the appearance of text. You can create a book specifically tailored for the recipient or a special occasion.

The current page layout of the book appears at the top in Page view.

⓾ Click the next page in the layout.

Note: *You can also click the right arrow (➡) at the bottom right corner of the interface to proceed to the next page.*

The Inside Flap page appears in the main viewing area.

⓫ Click the **Photos** button (🖼) to reveal the photos again.

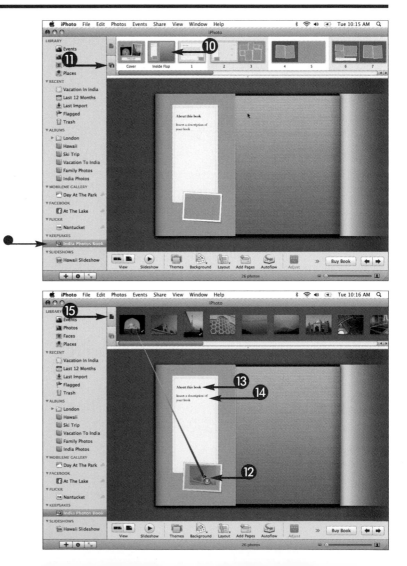

The photos appear.

⓬ Drag another photo from the photo browser into the drop zone in the template.

The photo fills the drop zone.

⓭ Click the **About this book** text and type **About the Photographer**.

Note: *Consider magnifying the page using the size slider (🔲) before typing your text.*

⓮ Click the **Insert a description of your book** field and type something about the photographer.

⓯ Click 🖼 .

● The page layout of the book appears in Page view.

16 Click the next page in the lineup.

The following page appears in the viewing area.

17 Edit the text in the title field.

18 Type a description of the book into the bottom field.

Note: You can progress through every page of the book in this manner until the book is complete. A book requires at least 20 pages.

*Note: You can click the **Themes** button ( ) at the bottom of the interface to change book themes.*

Can I change the front-to-back order of photos that overlap?

Yes. Some iPhoto themes, such as Scrapbook, use a design where photos appear to overlap on a page. To change the order, Control-click or right-click a photo and choose **Send to Back**.

Adjust Photos in a Book

You can make adjustments to exposure, highlights, and shadows, and even apply effects such as Black and White, Sepia, and Antique to any photo placed in the book. The ability to make adjustments to photos within the book enables you to not only fine-tune your photographs, but also to establish a unique look and feel.

Adjust Photos in a Book

1 Select a book in the Source list for which you want to adjust photographs.

2 Click ■.

The book layout appears in Page view.

3 Click the page that has the image you want to adjust.

The page opens in the main viewing area.

4 Click the photo that you want to adjust.

5 Click the **Adjust** button (■).

The Adjust panel opens.

6 Click **Sepia**.

7 Click ⊠ to close the Adjust panel.

Rearrange Photos in a Photo Book

You can rearrange two photos on the same page by dragging and dropping one directly on top of the other. Rearranging or swapping your photos enables you to find the perfect photo combination for the chosen book layout.

Rearrange Photos in a Photo Book

① Select the book in the Source list for which you want to rearrange photos.

② Click 📖.

The book layout appears in Page view.

③ Click the page that has multiple photos you want to rearrange.

The page opens in the main viewing area.

④ Click the photo that you want to move, drag it to the new position, and drop it on top of the picture.

The images swap positions.

Note: *You can see how your images work together by clicking the **Slideshow** button (▶ Slideshow) and viewing the book as a slideshow.*

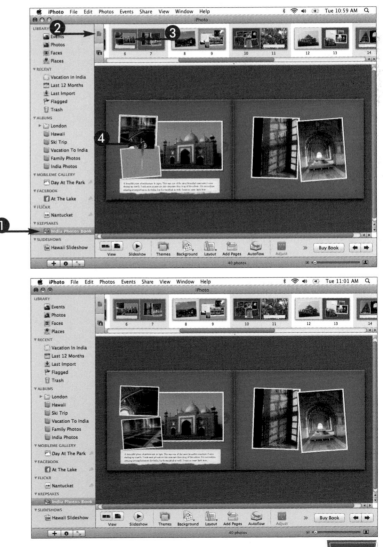

Move a Photo to a Different Page

You can move a photo to a new page by dragging and dropping in Page view. The ability to move a photo to a different page enables you to craft your story in perfect sequence.

Move a Photo to a Different Page

Note: *Moving photos to a different page will cause a reflow of subsequent photos, creating the need for additional adjustments to positioning.*

① Select the book in the Source list for which you want to move a photo to a different page.

② Click 🖼.

The book layout appears in Page view.

③ Click the page that has the photo you want to move.

The page opens in the main viewing area.

④ Click the photo that you want to move and drag it to the new page in the Page view.

The image is inserted into the new page and no longer appears on the previous page.

Note: *To remove a photo from a page, you can select it in the page and press* (Delete). *To delete it from the entire book, select it in the photo browser and press* (Delete).

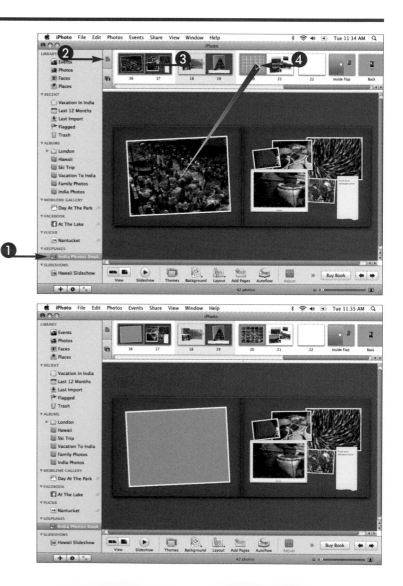

Add Photos to the Photo Browser

If you want to use photos that you previously did not select to use for the photo book, you can add them later to the photo browser. Adding photos to the photo browser enables you to take new photos and place them into a book already in progress.

Add Photos to the Photo Browser

① Click the group of images in the Source list that contains the photos you want to use.

② Select the photos that you want to use.

Note: *You can* ⌘ *-click to select multiple nonadjacent photos or drag a selection around adjacent photos.*

③ Drag the photos to the 🖼 in the Source list.

The photos are placed in the photo browser.

Note: *You can now click* 🖼 *to access the added photos in the book project.*

Edit the Book Layout

You can replace page layouts in the book with new ones. Editing the book layout enables you to find the perfect combination of photos for each page spread.

Edit the Book Layout

1. Select the book in the Source list for which you want to edit the book layout.

2. Click to open the book layout in Page view.

3. Click the page that you want to apply the new layout.

   The page appears in the main viewing area.

4. Click the **Layout** button ( ) and choose a category.

5. Click an option.

   The new layout is applied to the page.

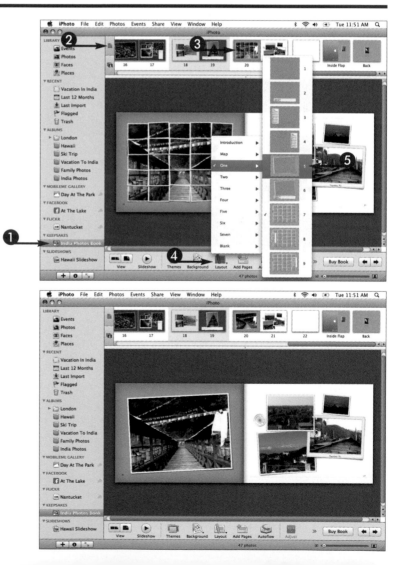

Add a New Book Page

You can add a new page to the existing pages of a photo book project, enabling you to increase the length of the book and use all of your favorite photos.

Add a New Book Page

① Select the book in the Source list for which you want to add a new book page.

② Click 📘.

The book layout appears in Page view.

③ Click the page that you want the new page to appear after.

④ Click the **Add Pages** button (Add Pages) and choose a category.

The new page is added.

Note: Refer to the "Edit the Book Layout" task in this chapter to see how to change the design of the page you just added.

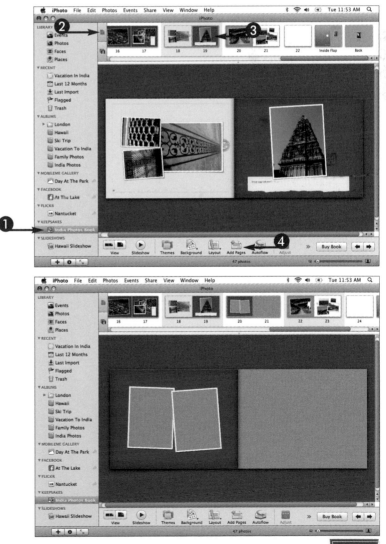

Change the Appearance of Text

iPhoto provides a number of options for changing the appearance of specific text in a book. You can change the font family, typeface, size, font color, and more, to personalize the text in your photo book to achieve design goals.

① Choose the photo book in the Source list that contains the text you want to style.

② Click 🖼️.

The book layout appears in Page view.

③ Click the page that contains the text you want to change.

The page appears in the main viewing window.

④ Click in the text field and highlight the text you want to change.

⑤ Click **Edit** in the main menu bar.

⑥ Click **Font**.

⑦ Click **Show Fonts**.

Note: You can also press ⌘ + T on the keyboard to open the Fonts panel.

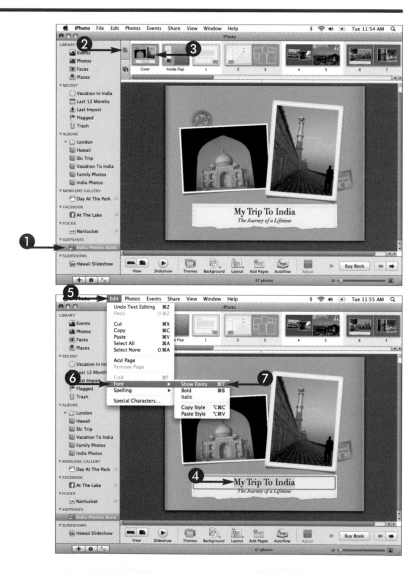

The Fonts panel opens.

8 Click a new font in the Family list.

The appearance of the text changes in the book template.

Note: *You can also use the slider on the far right to adjust the font size or type a new font size.*

9 Click to close the Fonts panel.

Why did a yellow text alert appear in the text field after I finished typing?

If a yellow text alert appears in the text field after you finish typing, the text may not fit in the field. You can reduce the font size, edit the text so that it contains fewer characters, or choose a new text style from the Fonts panel. Sometimes, iPhoto may display a text alert even if the text fits. If this happens, change the font. If you are set on using a particular font, you can print a test page to see if it prints properly.

Change Default Text Settings

You can change the overall default text for an entire book, rather than specified text only. Changing default text enables you to make overall changes to the text in a project to accomplish your design goals.

① Choose the photo book in the Source list that contains the text you want to change.

② Click the **Settings** button ().

Note: If you do not see the 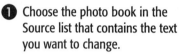, click the double arrows that appear in the toolbar and choose **Settings**.

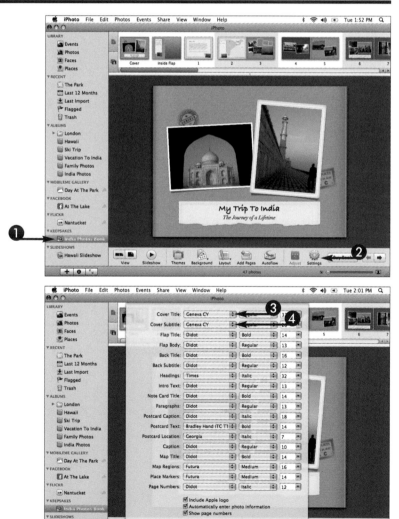

The Settings options appear.

③ Click the **Cover Title** ⬍ and choose a new font family.

④ Click the **Cover Subtitle** ⬍ and choose a font family.

⑤ Click the **Flap Body**  and choose a font family.

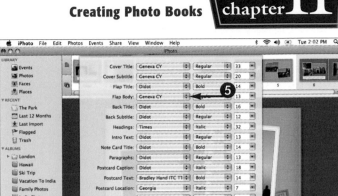

⑥ Click the **Intro Text** and choose a new font family.

⑦ Click **OK**.

The changes to text are updated in the book.

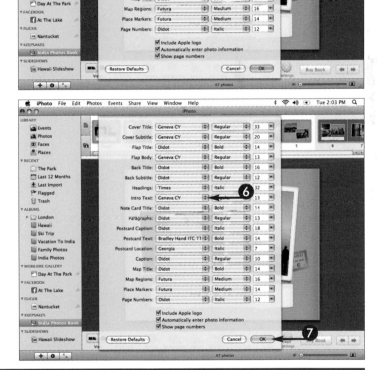

TIP

Does changing the default text settings change the text for all photo books I have created?
No. When you change the default text settings, you are changing the settings for that particular book only. Changing the default settings is a convenient way to change the text in your entire document from one location instead of going to each individual page and implementing the changes. If you do not like the changes you have made, you can restore all text to its original appearance by clicking **Restore Defaults**.

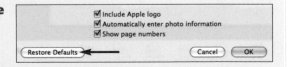

Add a Map to a Book

You can add a map to a photo book that shows the geographical area in which photos were taken, and edit the map to add or remove locations. Each book theme offers a map page layout, and the Travel theme offers a variety of map options. A map can be added to any page except for the front and back covers or dustcover of a hardcover book.

Add a Map

① Choose the photo book in the Source list to which you want to add a map.

The book chosen in this example is in the Travel theme.

② Click ▣.

The page layout appears in Page view.

③ Select the page that you want to replace with a map.

④ Click ▦.

⑤ Click **Map** and then choose a map layout from the menu.

The page is replaced with the map. iPhoto detects the location information for the photos and automatically places pins on the map for the various locations.

Note: The Travel theme has more map options than other themes.

Note: If your photos were not taken with a GPS-enabled camera, go to Chapter 3 to see how to add location information to photos.

6 Click the map to make the map editing pane appear.

7 Click in a check box to uncheck and hide locations on the map.

Note: You can also click the Plus (+) and Minus buttons (-) to zoom in and out of the map.

8 Click in the map and drag it to frame the region you want to appear.

9 Slide the zoom slider to the right to zoom into the map.

10 Click in the **Title** field and type a name for the map.

The name appears in the bottom left corner of the map.

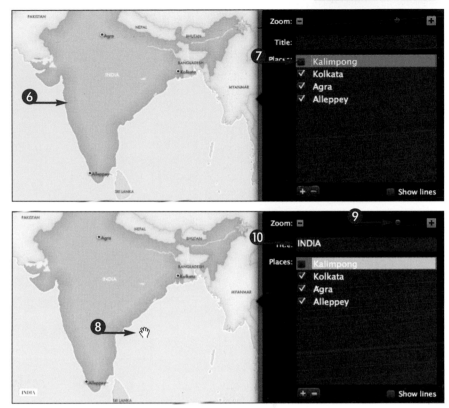

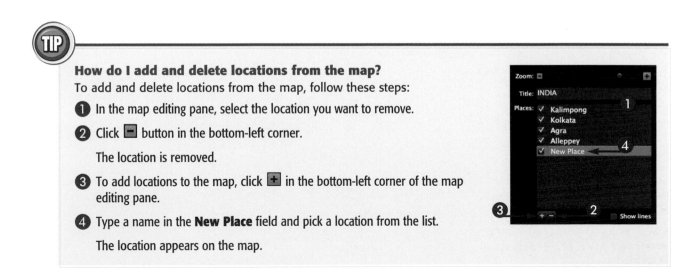

TIP

How do I add and delete locations from the map?
To add and delete locations from the map, follow these steps:

1 In the map editing pane, select the location you want to remove.

2 Click button in the bottom-left corner.

The location is removed.

3 To add locations to the map, click in the bottom-left corner of the map editing pane.

4 Type a name in the **New Place** field and pick a location from the list.

The location appears on the map.

Create Direction Lines on a Map

You can create direction lines on a map to depict your travels from one location to another. You can change the direction of lines by changing the order of the locations listed in the map editing pane. Adding direction lines on a map is a great way to personalize your story.

Create Direction Lines on a Map

1 Choose the photo book in the Source list that contains the map.

2 Click 📖.

The page layout appears.

3 Click the page spread in the Page view that has the map.

● The map appears in the main viewing area.

4 Click in the map to open the map editing pane.

5 Click the **Show Lines** option (☐ changes to ☑).

● Direction lines appear in the map.

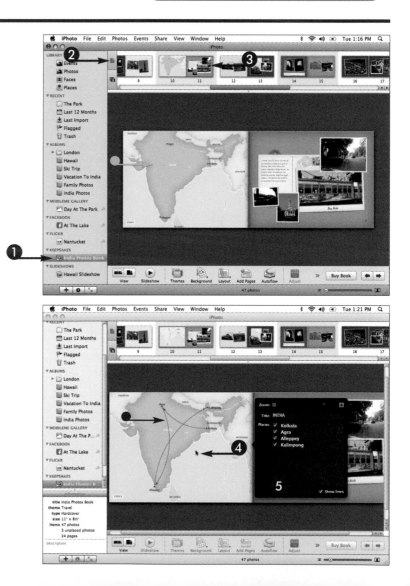

6 Select all locations in the map editing pane that do not pertain to the particular region of focus in the map.

7 Click 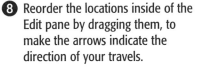.

The nonrelevant locations on the map are removed.

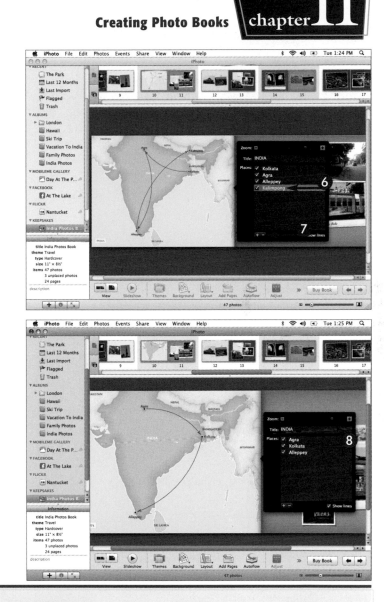

8 Reorder the locations inside of the Edit pane by dragging them, to make the arrows indicate the direction of your travels.

Note: *Make your starting point first in the list. Drag your next destination into the second spot on the list, and so on.*

The arrows depict your travels across the region in sequence.

TIPS

How do I close the map editing pane after I have finished creating my direction lines in the map?

When you are finished editing the locations within the map, you can close the map editing pane by clicking an empty space surrounding the pane, or by clicking another page in the book.

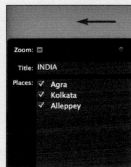

Does deleting locations in the map editing pane delete the locations from my photo in the Library?

No. When you delete locations in the map editing pane, you are deleting it only from that map, not from your photos, other maps, or Events.

Order a Photo Book

You can click Buy Book to order professionally made copies of your book over the Internet. Once you have set up your Apple ID and a 1-Click account, you can have a professionally bound photo book delivered to your door or to a friend or family member. A professionally bound book of your photos can make a great gift.

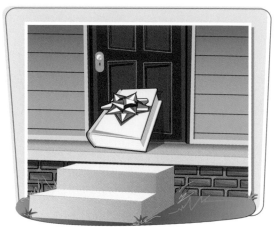

Order a Photo Book

Note: *Make sure that you review your book closely to see that it is exactly the way you want it before placing an order.*

① Choose the photo book in the Source list that you want to order.

② Click **Buy Book**.

● iPhoto may alert you that it detects low-resolution photos that are not optimal for the print size of the book. iPhoto also warns you if any default text fields have not been edited. You can choose to Cancel and correct the problem or click **OK** to proceed.

If you already have an Apple ID and have set up a 1-Click account, the Order Book window opens.

Note: *Click Setup to set up an account if you have never placed an order before. If you have an Apple account, enter your ID and password to set up a 1-Click account.*

③ Click the **Quantity** ⬦ and choose a quantity from the pop-up menu.

④ Click the **Ship To** ⬦ and specify a shipping address from the pop-up menu.

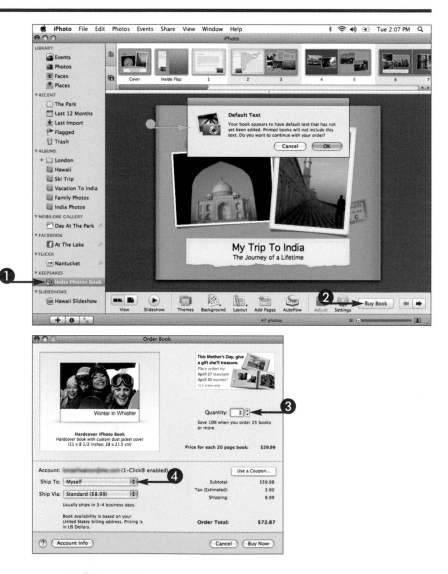

chapter 11

⑤ Click the **Ship Via** 🔽 and choose a shipping method from the pop-up menu.

⑥ Review the order form to see if it is correct.

⑦ Click **Buy Now** to place the order.

TIPS

How do I edit my shipping information?

You can edit the shipping information by clicking **Account Info** at the bottom of the Order Book window. For your protection, you need to enter your account password if you are not signed in. The Account Info window opens and you can edit the shipping information as well as billing information.

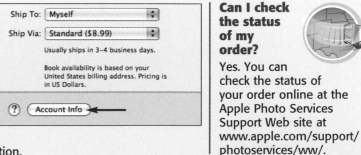

Can I check the status of my order?

Yes. You can check the status of your order online at the Apple Photo Services Support Web site at www.apple.com/support/photoservices/ww/.

Creating Photo Calendars and Cards

iPhoto makes it easy for you to create beautiful photo calendars, greeting cards, and post cards. You can switch between professionally designed themes for both calendars and cards, add your own special dates to calendars, and customize your greetings to create the perfect gift for a friend or family member. After you have finished building your project, you can have professional prints made by ordering online, then have them delivered.

Create a
Calendar

iPhoto enables you to create high-quality photo calendars that can contain from as few as 12 months up to 24 months. Using a variety of professionally designed themes to create calendars of your favorite photographs can make an excellent gift for friends and family members.

Create a Calendar

1 Select the group of photos that you want to use in the calendar from the Source list.

2 Click the **Calendar** button (⬜).

Note: Based on the resolution of your screen, or if your iPhoto window is less than 1024 pixels in width, you may need to click **Keepsakes** (🖼️), and then click the Calendar button (⬜) as seen in this example.

Note: You can also click the **Plus** button (➕) in the bottom left of the interface and then choose **Calendar**.

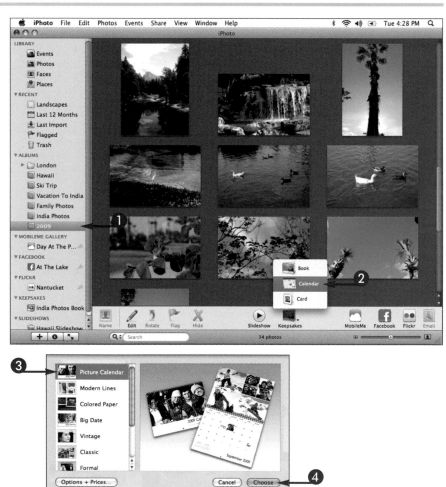

The themes dialog appears.

3 Click a theme from the list.

A preview of the theme appears to the right.

4 Click **Choose**.

A dialog opens, prompting you to specify the calendar details.

5 Click the **Start calendar on** and choose the month on which the calendar is to begin.

6 Click the year field and choose the year for the calendar.

7 Click the **Months** and choose how many months will be represented in the calendar.

8 Click the **Show national holidays** to choose a country from the menu.

9 Click **OK**.

A dialog opens, informing you that you can drag photos from the photo browser into the pages or use Autoflow.

10 Click **OK**.

11 Drag a photo from the photo browser and drop it in the calendar page.

The photo is inserted into the page.

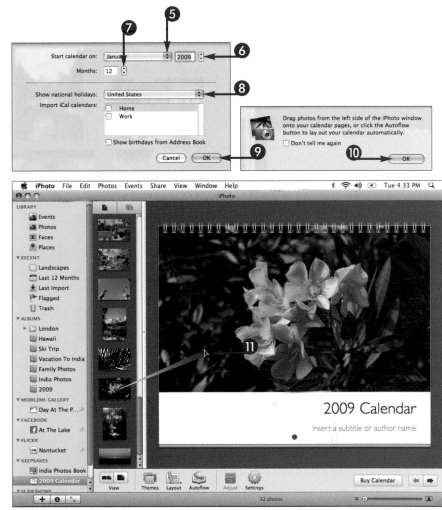

Can I add special information to a specific date in the calendar?
Yes. You can add information directly to a date in the calendar. You can click the date onto which you want to add the information and then type the information into the text box that opens. Click to close the text box after you are finished.

continued

Create a
Calendar *(continued)*

You can personalize the text within photo calendars to accommodate your specific needs. iPhoto makes it easy for you to navigate from page to page dragging and dropping new photos into the template as you go.

⑫ Click in the title text at the bottom and type a new title.

⑬ Click in the subtitle field and type a subtitle or name.

⑭ Click the **Page View** button ().

The page layout of the entire calendar appears.

⑮ Click the next page in the list.

Note: You can also use the right arrow in the bottom right of the interface to proceed to the next calendar month.

The new page appears in the main viewing area.

⑯ Click the Photo browser button (🖼).

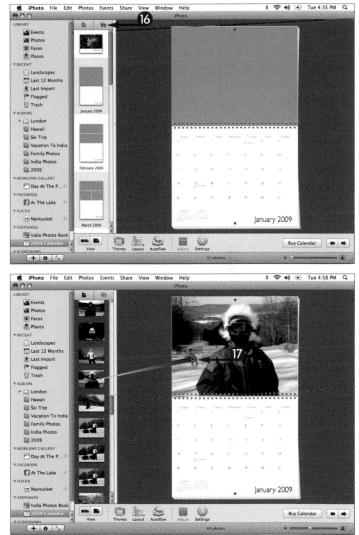

All of the photos associated with the calendar project appear.

⑰ Drag a photo from the photo browser onto the calendar page.

The photo is inserted onto the calendar page.

Note: *You can use this same method to add photos to the pages in the rest of the calendar.*

 TIP

How do I add photos in specific dates in the calendar?
You can add photos directly to specific dates in the calendar by simply dragging a photograph from the photo browser and dropping it onto the date. The photo is resized and placed into the date square.

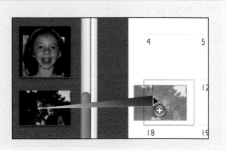

Change Calendar Months

You can change the starting month and the number of months in a calendar during a project. Changing calendar months enables you to customize the calendar for your particular project.

1 Choose the calendar project in the Source list for which you want to change the months.

2 Click the **Settings** button (⚙).

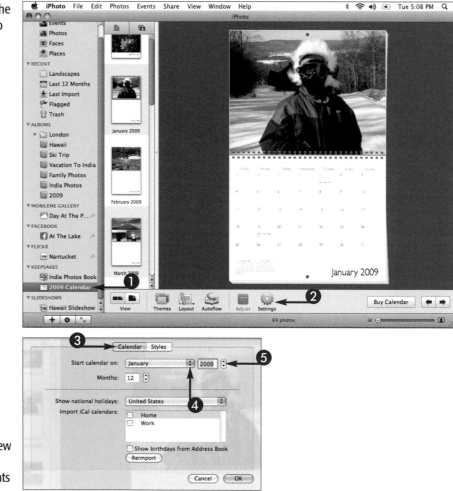

The settings options appear.

3 Click **Calendar**.

4 Click the **Start calendar on** ⬍ and choose a month from the pop-up menu.

5 Click the year field and type a new year, or click ⬍ to change the value in the text box in increments of one year.

6 Click the **Months** field and type the number of months, or click 🔃 to adjust the value in the text box in increments.

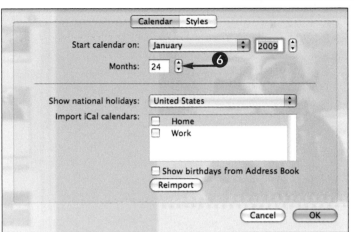

7 Click **OK**.

The changes are updated in the calendar.

Can I include holidays in my calendar at this point?
Yes. If you originally did not choose to include holidays in the calendar, you can add holidays in the calendar settings. You can choose a country in the Show national holidays field to display that country's holidays. You also have an option to import important dates from your iCal Calendars.

Change the Appearance of Calendar Text

iPhoto provides a number of options for you to change the appearance of specific text in a calendar project. In the Fonts panel, you can change the font type, typeface, size, font color, and more to personalize the text in your photo book to achieve design goals.

Change the Appearance of Calendar Text

① Choose the calendar in the Source list that contains the text you want to style.

② Click 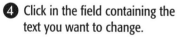.

The calendar layout appears in Page view.

③ Click the calendar page that contains the text you want to change.

The calendar page appears in the main viewing window.

④ Click in the field containing the text you want to change.

Note: If the text is in a date square, click on the date square to open the text box.

⑤ Highlight the text.

⑥ Click **Edit** in the main menu bar.

⑦ Click **Font**.

⑧ Click **Show Fonts**.

Note: You can also press ⌘ + T to open the Fonts panel.

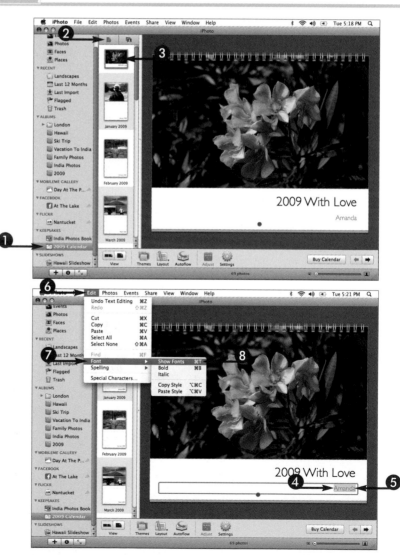

The Fonts panel opens.

9 Click a new font family.

The appearance of the text changes in the calendar template.

10 Click a new text size.

Note: *you can also use the slider on the far right to adjust the font size.*

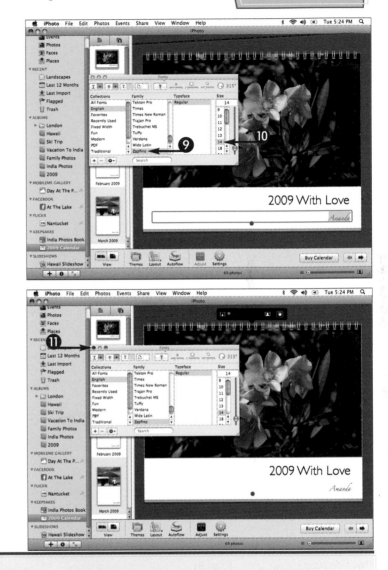

The font size changes in the calendar field.

11 Click to close the Fonts panel.

Why did a yellow text alert appear in the text field after I finished typing?

A yellow text alert means that the text probably does not fit into the text field. You can reduce the font size, edit the text so that it contains fewer words, or you can choose a new text style from the Fonts window.

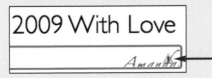

How do I run a spell check in iPhoto?

Words that iPhoto believes are misspelled are underlined in red. Control -click or right-click the word and choose the correct spelling. You can also highlight words and go to Edit > Spelling > Check Spelling.

2009 With Luv

Amanda

Change Default Text Settings for a Calendar

You can change the overall default text for an entire calendar rather than specified text only. Changing default text enables you to make overall changes to the text in a project to achieve a desired look and feel.

1 Choose the calendar project in the Source list that contains the text you want to change.

2 Click .

The settings options appear.

3 Click **Styles**.

The style options appear.

④ Click the **Cover Title** ⬍ and choose a new font family from the pop-up menu.

⑤ Click the **Cover Subtitle** ⬍ and change the font family from the pop-up menu.

Cover Title:	Zapfino	Regular	42
Cover Subtitle:	Zapfino	Regular	22
Page Text:	Gill Sans	Regular	Choose font style for
Comments:	Gill Sans	Light	8
iCal Events:	Gill Sans	Light	8
Photo Captions:	Gill Sans	Light	8

☑ Include Apple logo   (Restore Defaults)

(Cancel)   (OK)

⑥ Click **OK**.

The changes are updated in the calendar.

Cover Title:	Zapfino	Regular	42
Cover Subtitle:	Zapfino	Regular	22
Page Text:	Gill Sans	Regular	10.5
Comments:	Gill Sans	Light	8
iCal Events:	Gill Sans	Light	8
Photo Captions:	Gill Sans	Light	8

☑ Include Apple logo   (Restore Defaults)

(Cancel)   (OK) ← ⑥

TIP

If I change the default text setting, will the text in my other calendar projects be changed?
No. When you change the default text settings for a calendar project, only that calendar is affected. Changing the default settings is a convenient way to change the text in your entire calendar from one location instead of going to each individual page and making the changes. You can click **Restore Defaults** to restore all text to its original appearance.

Move a Photo to a Different Calendar Page

You can move a photo to a new calendar page by dragging and dropping it into the page in Page view. The ability to move a photo to a different calendar page helps you to find the perfect sequence of photos.

① Select the calendar project in the Source list for which you want to move photos.

② Click ▣.

The calendar layout appears in Page view.

③ Click the calendar page that has the photo you want to move.

The page opens in the main viewing area.

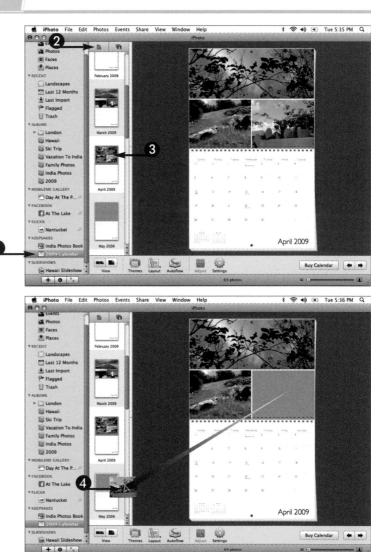

④ Click the photo that you want to move and drag it to the new page in the Page view.

The image is inserted into the new calendar page and it no longer appears on the previous page.

Note: *To remove a photo from a page, you can select it in the page, and then press* Delete *. To delete it from the entire calendar project, select it in the photo browser and then press* Delete *.*

You can swap photos on the same page by dragging and dropping one directly on top of the other. Rearranging or swapping your photos enables you to find the best photo combination for the chosen calendar page.

Rearrange Photos in a Calendar

① Select the calendar project in the Source list for which you want to rearrange the photos.

② Click [].

The calendar layout appears in Page view.

③ Click the calendar page that has multiple photos you want to rearrange.

The page opens in the main viewing area.

④ Click and drag the photo you want to move and drop it on another photograph.

The photographs swap positions.

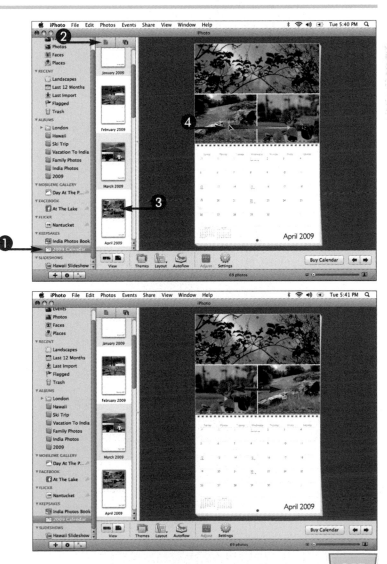

Customize Photos on Dates

You can make edits such as enlarging and reframing scenes in photos placed on dates in the calendar. You can also add captions to photos on dates and specify the location of the caption. The ability to customize photos on dates enables you to make certain days very special.

① Choose the calendar project in the Source list for which you want to customize photos on dates.

② Click 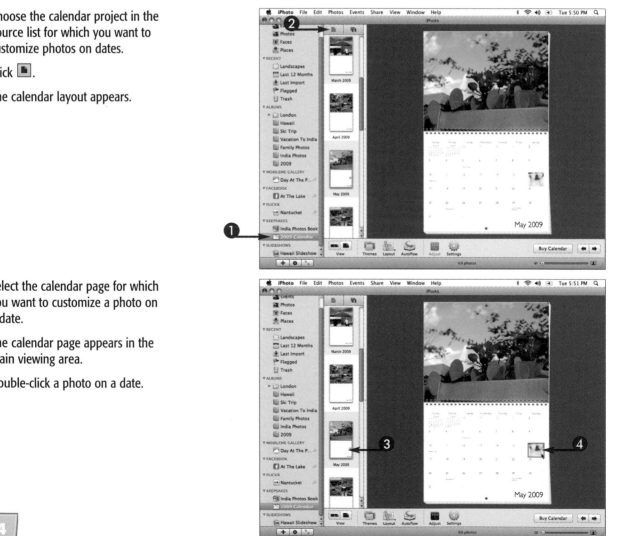.

The calendar layout appears.

③ Select the calendar page for which you want to customize a photo on a date.

The calendar page appears in the main viewing area.

④ Double-click a photo on a date.

The photo opens with a caption box.

5 Use the zoom slider to enlarge or shrink the picture.

6 Click in the caption field and type a new caption.

Note: The default caption is the name of the photo.

7 Click the **Caption** option to make the caption visible in the calendar (changes to).

8 Click one of the arrows to determine the position of the caption.

Note: Your choices are to the left of the photo, above the photo, to the right of the photo, or below the photo.

The caption was placed above the photo in this example.

9 Click here to close the caption box.

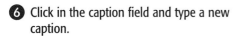

TIP

Do you have any suggestions on writing captions?

You are dealing with limited space, so keep captions short and sweet to around two or three words; for example, Robyn's Birthday or Happy Birthday, Mom. If the caption is too long it can consume a large amount of real estate in other date fields. The text will also be small on the printed calendar, and a small paragraph may be hard to read.

Adjust Photos in a Calendar

You can make adjustments to exposure, highlights, and shadows, and even apply effects such as Black and White, Sepia, and Antique to any photo placed inside of a calendar. The ability to adjust photos within a calendar enables you to not only fine-tune your photographs but also to establish a unique look and feel.

Adjust Photos in a Calendar

1 Select a calendar in the Source list for which you want to adjust photographs.

2 Click ▣ to open the calendar layout in Page view.

3 Click the calendar page that has images you want to adjust.

4 Click the photo inside of the calendar that you want to adjust.

● Controls appear above the photo you selected.

5 Click the **Adjust** button (▣).

The Adjust panel opens.

6 Click **B & W**.

7 Click ⊗ to close the Adjust panel.

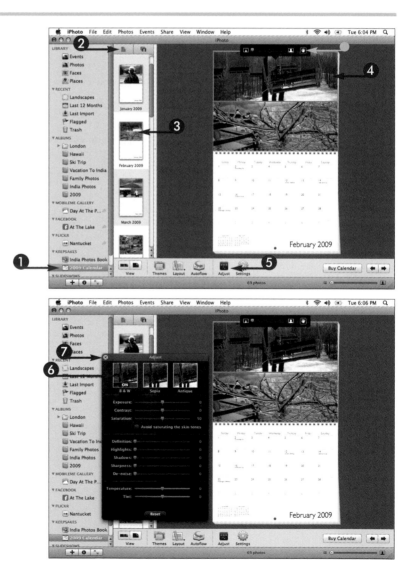

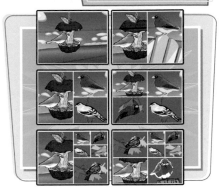

You can replace current pages in the calendar with new ones. Editing the calendar layout helps you to achieve the best photo combination and sequence for each calendar month.

❶ Select the calendar project in the Source list for which you want to edit the layout.

❷ Click 🖻 to open the calendar layout in Page view.

❸ Click the calendar page to which you want to apply a new layout.

❹ Click the **Layout** button (🖳) and choose a category.

Note: *The page options are listed by number of photos per page.*

❺ Click the layout option.

● The page is shown with the new layout.

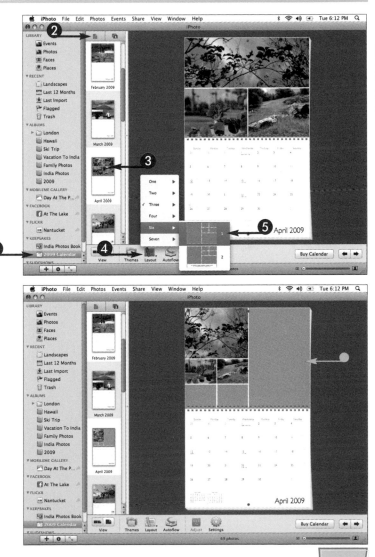

Import Dates from Your iCal Calendar

You can import your important dates from your iCal calendar into your iPhoto calendar. The ability to import dates from your iCal calendar saves you the time from entering them manually within your iPhoto calendar.

① Choose the calendar project in the Source list for which you want to import the iCal dates.

② Click .

The settings options appear.

③ Click the **Calendar** tab.

④ In the Import iCal calendars
section, choose one or more
iCal calendars for import
(☐ changes to ☑).

⑤ Click **OK**.

The iCal dates are imported into
the iPhoto calendar.

What if I do not see anything in the Import iCal calendars field?

If you cannot see the calendars you have created in iPhoto inside
the Import iCal calendars field, click **Reimport**. If the calendars
still do not appear, you may not have any saved dates in iCal.
Check in your iCal calendar to see if you indeed have saved
dates and refer to the iCal help topics in the iCal main menu bar.

Order Your Photo Calendar

You can click Buy Calendar to order professionally made copies of your photo calendar over the Internet. Once you have set up your Apple ID and 1-Click account, you can have a professionally printed calendar of your photos delivered to your door or to a friend or family member. A professionally printed calendar of your photos can make a great gift.

Note: *Make sure that you review your calendar closely to see if it is exactly the way you want it before placing an order.*

1 In the Source list, choose the calendar that you want to order.

2 Click **Buy Calendar**.

● iPhoto may alert you if it detects low-resolution photos in the project that are not optimal for the print size of the calendar. iPhoto also warns you if there are any default text fields that have not been edited. You can choose **Cancel** and then replace the photos, or choose **OK** to proceed.

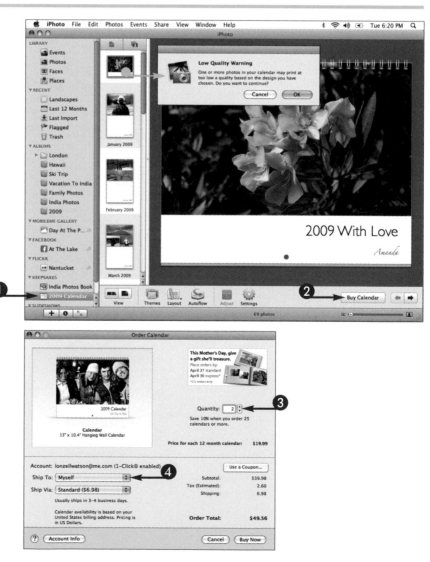

If you already have an Apple ID and have set up a 1-Click account, the Order Calendar dialog opens.

Note: *Click **Setup** to set up an account if you have never placed an order before. If you have an Apple account, enter your ID and password to set up a 1-Click account.*

3 Click 🔼 and choose a quantity.

4 Click the **Ship To** 🔼 to specify a shipping address from the pop-up menu.

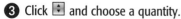

⑤ Click the **Ship Via** 🔼 and choose a shipping method from the pop-up menu.

⑥ Review the order form to see if it is correct.

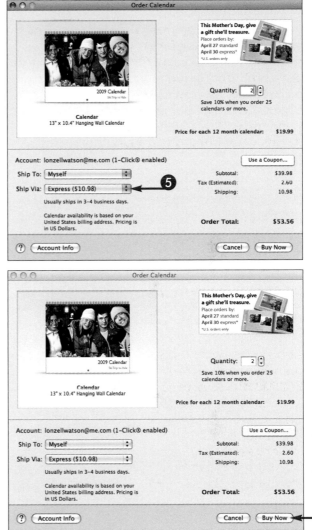

⑦ Click **Buy Now** to place the order.

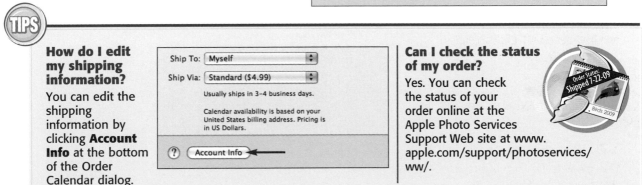

TIPS

How do I edit my shipping information?
You can edit the shipping information by clicking **Account Info** at the bottom of the Order Calendar dialog.

Can I check the status of my order?
Yes. You can check the status of your order online at the Apple Photo Services Support Web site at www. apple.com/support/photoservices/ ww/.

Create a Greeting Card and Post Card

iPhoto creates 5x7 greeting cards and 4x6 post cards. The greeting cards are of the folding variety and either fold at the top, when using a horizontal picture, or on the left side when using a vertical photograph. All cards are complete with envelopes. Creating personalized gift cards and post cards is easy in iPhoto, and is a great sentimental gesture to friends and family.

Create a Greeting Card and Post Card

1 Select one or more photos to use in the card.

Note: *Some designs are made to require multiple photographs on the outside and inside the card.*

2 Click the **Card** button (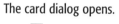) at the bottom of the interface.

Note: *Based on the width of your iPhoto window, if your iPhoto window is less than 1024 pixels in width, you may need to click ▣ and then click the Card button (▣) as seen in this example.*

The card dialog opens.

3 Click ⬍ Choose which type of card you want to create.

Your choice appears in the preview area.

4 Choose a card category.

The choices for the card category appear in the preview area.

5 Choose a card theme.

Your selection is depicted in the preview area.

6 Click **Choose**.

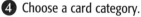

iPhoto switches to Card view with the outside of the card on the left and the inside of the card on the right.

iPhoto populates the card with photos you have designated and the card project appears in the Source list.

7 Click and drag a new photo from the photo browser and place it into the card.

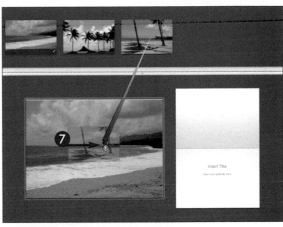

● The new photo replaces the one placed by iPhoto.

TIPS

How do I add other photos to the card project?

You can add more photos to the card project by selecting a group of photos in the Source list and dragging them to the card project icon (🔲) in the Source list. The photos then appear in the photo browser at the top of the Card view. You can then drag the photo from the photo browser and place it into the card template.

How do I rearrange photos in a card theme that uses more than one photograph?

You can rearrange multiple photos by dropping one on top of the other; iPhoto swaps the positions of the photographs.

Add Text to a Card

Each card template includes text fields where you can add your own personalized message. Greeting cards enable you to add text on the inside of the box, whereas post cards offer a block of text on the back of the card and are complete with a "postage here" box.

① Select the card project in the Source list for which you want to add or edit the text.

② Click in the **Insert Title** text field and type a new title.

Note: Consider magnifying the card using the size slider before you type a greeting.

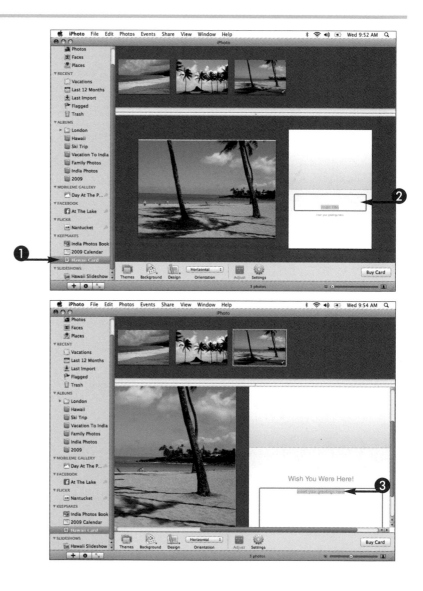

③ Click in the **Insert your greetings here** field and type a greeting.

Note: Words that iPhoto believes are misspelled are underlined in red. You can Control -click or right-click the underlined word and choose a suggestion for the word in the menu.

Note: You can highlight the text and click **Edit** in the main menu bar and choose Font and then choose Show Fonts to change the appearance of the text.

You can make adjustments to exposure, highlights, and shadows, and even apply effects such as Black and White, Sepia, and Antique to any photo placed inside of a card. The ability to make adjustments to photos within a card enables you to not only fine-tune your photographs but also to establish a unique look and feel.

Adjust Photos in a Card

① Select a card in the Source list for which you want to adjust photographs.

The card appears in the main viewing area.

② Click the photo that you want to adjust.

● Controls appear above the photo you selected and the Adjust icon becomes active at the bottom of the interface.

③ Click ▦.

The Adjust panel opens.

④ Drag the temperature slider to adjust the photograph.

Note: *Adjust any way that you deem necessary for your particular photo.*

In this example, a little extra warmth was added to the beach scene.

⑤ Click ⊗ to close the Adjust panel.

Order Your Cards

You can click Buy Card to order professionally made copies of your cards on the Internet. Once you have set up your Apple ID and 1-Click account, you can have professionally printed cards delivered to your door or to a friend or family member. Professionally printed greeting cards and post cards can make a great gift for friends and family.

Note: *Make sure that you review your card closely to see if it is exactly the way you want it before placing an order.*

① In the Source list, choose the card project that you want to order.

② Click **Buy Card**.

If you already have an Apple ID and have set up a 1-Click account, the Order Card dialog opens.

Note: *Click **Setup** to set up an account if you have never placed an order before. If you have an Apple account, enter your ID and password to set up a 1-Click account.*

③ Click the **Quantity** 🔼 to adjust the number value in the text box, or click in the Quantity field and type a new quantity.

④ Click the **Ship To** 🔼 to specify a shipping address from the pop-up menu.

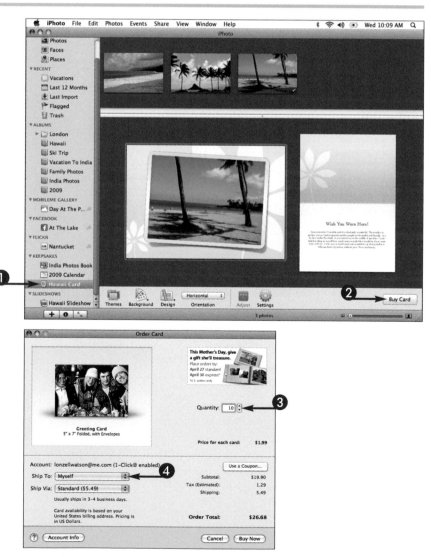

⑤ Click the **Ship Via** ⬍ and choose a shipping method from the pop-up menu.

⑥ Review the order to see if it is correct.

⑦ Click **Buy Now** to place the order.

How do I edit my shipping information?
You can edit the shipping information by clicking **Account Info** at the bottom of the Order Card dialog. For your protection, you need to enter your account password if you are not signed in. The Account Info dialog opens and you can edit the shipping information as well as billing information.

| Ship To: | Myself |
| Ship Via: | Express ($7.99) |

Usually ships in 3-4 business days.

Card availability is based on your United States billing address. Pricing is in US Dollars.

(?) Account Info ⟵

Can I check the status of my order?
Yes. You can check the status of your order online at the Apple Photo Services Support Web site at www.apple.com/support/photoservices/ww/.

CHAPTER 13

Memory Cards and Storage

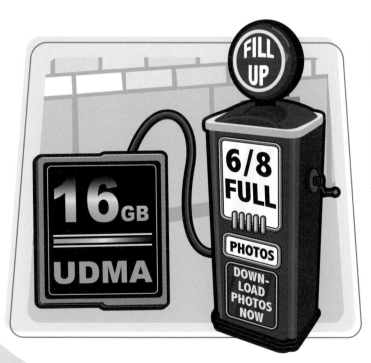

Memory cards and storage devices are essential components to the digital photographer. Understanding the various options for memory cards, storage devices, and how to properly care for them is as important as knowing how to operate your camera.

Memory Cards and Memory Card Readers

The memory cards that you use for your digital camera are the digital equivalent to film. Digital cameras capture photo image data and store it to a memory card. Depending on the size of the memory card and the format of the images, a memory card could hold just a few images to hundreds of images. The quality and proper care of your memory cards play an important role in the longevity of your photo files.

Memory Cards

Each camera accepts different types of memory cards including CompactFlash (CF), Secure Digital (SD), Secure Digital High Capacity (SDHC), Memory Stick (MS), MultiMedia Card (MMC), and xD Picture Card (xD). Each card also comes in various speeds and storage capacities (megabytes or gigabytes).

Brand Name Imposters

Relabeled and repackaged memory cards do exist in the market, so buyers beware. These cards may appear to be the real thing, but their quality is inferior. The storage capacity may not be what is marked, and they may have incorrect partitioning which can lead to card corruption. Buy memory cards only from known vendors that you trust. It does not matter how great your camera is if the memory card fails.

Download with Memory Card Readers

Using a card reader to download photos to your computer is faster, safer, and more convenient than connecting the camera to a computer for download. Using a card reader may help to avoid wear and tear on camera terminals. It also frees up the camera during the download process so that you can continue shooting with another card. Card readers also help you save battery power.

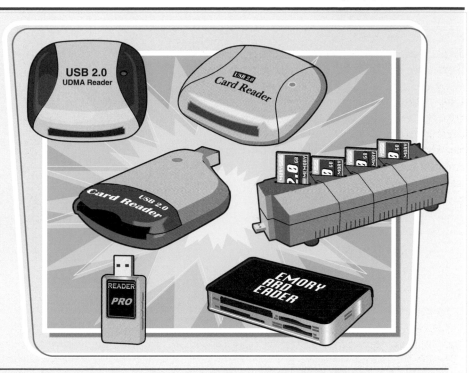

Use Multiple Card Readers

Memory card readers connect to a computer by way of USB or FireWire cable and mount as an external device. Using a UDMA (Ultra Direct Memory Access) reader with a UDMA card enables you to take advantage of faster transfer times. You can buy card readers with single slots or many slots. Multi-card readers provide slots that can accept different types of cards, and multi-slot readers enable you to download from several cards at a time.

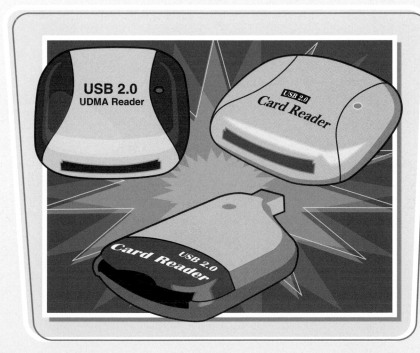

Using Memory Cards Properly

A memory card is an electronic device and is susceptible to corruption. The first line of defense in protecting the images on a memory card is to always buy brand-name memory cards from reputable vendors that you trust. This decreases your chance of buying fake memory cards that appear to be brand name. There are things you can do to protect the image files on your memory card and avoid most problems, if you follow a few simple guidelines while using them.

Memory Card Type, Speed, and Capacity

Many manufacturers, including the manufacturers of cameras, produce memory cards. The type of memory card that you need for your camera can depend on the camera manufacturer. In general, a card with a higher speed enables you to take consecutive shots more quickly because the image is written to the card faster. You can choose a memory card by the largest amount of RAW or JPEG files it can hold. The higher the capacity of the memory card the more photos you are able to take. For safety purposes, having a collection of memory cards with smaller capacities may be safer than taking one card with a large capacity on a trip, if the one high-capacity card proves to be defective or corrupt.

Format and Reformat the Card in the Camera

Do not format your memory cards in any device other than the camera in which it will be used. Each camera has its own system and file structure. To format the memory card, insert it into the camera and choose the camera's Format setting within the camera menu system. When asked if you would like to erase the data on the card, choose Yes to format the card. Periodically reformat your memory card to maintain its level of performance.

Insert and Remove Cards Safely

Make sure that the camera is turned off when you insert or remove a memory card. Never remove a card from the camera, or card reader, or disconnect the cable from the card reader, while data is being written to or from the memory card. Never take a partially filled card and insert it into another camera because it can result in the loss of your photos. In general, do not force a memory card into the camera or card reader.

Avoid Filling Up a Memory Card

Generally it is safer to leave some space on the card, about two images worth, at the end of each card. If the card is full and you take a picture and there is not enough room to write the last file, the card may become corrupted.

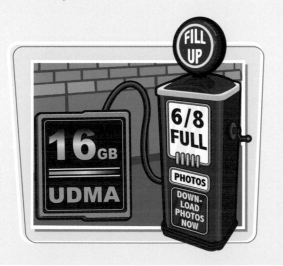

Do Not Switch Off the Camera Too Quickly

If your camera has a burst or continuous shooting mode, make sure that you do not remove the card too quickly just after shooting. When shooting many images quickly, as in these modes, the camera needs more time to write all of the data to the memory card. If you switch off the camera before it is finished writing the data to the card, you will lose images.

Keep Memory Cards Dry and Clean

Make sure that your memory cards never get wet and that they are stored in an environment with a controlled temperature. Consider storing unused cards in a plastic casing for an extra layer of protection.

External Hard Drives for Storage

The number of images that you acquire through digital photography grows dramatically. iPhoto does a great job keeping your photos organized, but you still need a plan to store the electronic images once they are downloaded from the camera. You need the storage capability that enables you to back up and archive photos. Understanding the difference between storage, backup, and archiving helps you better devise a strategy to locate and secure your digital photographs.

Storage

Storage generally refers to a permanent mass storage device, such as a computer hard disk drive where you can download and save electronic data and retrieve it. RAM is a form of computer data storage. Unlike a hard disk drive, it forgets what was stored on it when the computer shuts down.

Storage Drive

A storage drive can be internal or external and is a computer storage device that can store your digital files and make them accessible. A storage drive with a large capacity enables you to store a growing number of the digital photographs you use in iPhoto. An external drive enables you to add to the storage capacity of a computer, if there is not room to install a drive internally. External storage can also include DVDs, CDs, flash drives, and network drives.

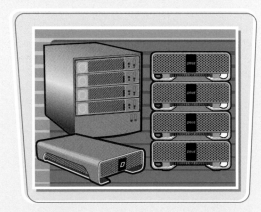

Backup

Backup is generally a safety precaution, which refers to making copies of data so that the copies can be used to restore the original files in the case of file corruption or data loss after a hard drive failure. The backup copies often include several versions of the edited files. When you back up, you are making copies, and not removing the original files from their original locations.

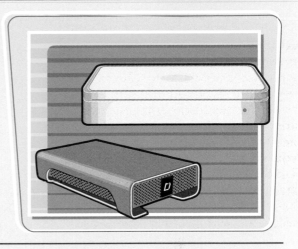

Backup Software

Backup software is a computer program used to automate the process of copying original files for backup. Backup software also simplifies the process of restoring files from the original storage if the original storage device should fail. EMC Retrospect and Time Machine work in the background of your Mac computer and automatically make duplicates of important files at specified intervals.

Archive

An archive consists of the finalized digital images comprising a photographer's body of work. Along with photos, you can archive financial records and other miscellaneous documents that need to be saved for future retrieval. Archived files do not need to be accessed regularly, but are generally organized so that they can be easily searched. Archives can be stored on DVDs, CDs, and internal or external drives, and are kept in a separate, secure location for security purposes.

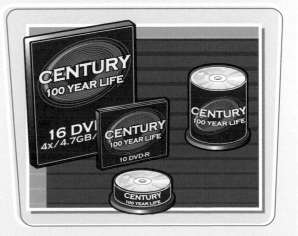

Types of External Hard Drives

External hard drives come in many different shapes and storage capacities, and with various different connection types and configurations. There are single drives, photo-specific options that enable you to copy, store, and view photos on memory cards, and various RAID (Redundant Array of Independent Disks) options. iPods are also handy for transporting photos and are well integrated for slideshows.

Hard Drive Options

External hard drives are great options for storage, backup, and archiving photographs. The rotational speed of the disks in the drive plays a big role in the performance of the drive. The typical household drive ranges from 5400–7200 RPMs. Options for single drives include the G-Drive and G-Drive Q. RAID-type hard drive options include the G-safe and the G-RAID Mini (g-technology.com).

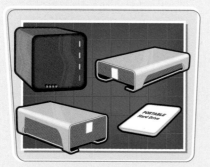

Drive Connections

The most common hard drive connections are USB2, FireWire 400, and FireWire 800. In general, the USB2 drives cost less, in turn making them the most available on the market. FireWire drives handle data transfers more efficiently and are better for when you need to constantly access the drive. Some drives come equipped with USB2 and FireWire 400 and 800 connections, such as the G-Drive mini Triple. eSata connections are newer and have a faster read and write speed than both USB and FireWire connections. Only the MacPro has a slot where you can add an eSATA card.

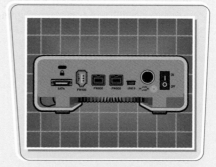

Small Drives For Travel

The smaller format hard drives are great for portable use, especially if you have a laptop. Small drives such as the Iomega eGo Helium Portable hard drive are thin in design and can be easily slipped into a purse, briefcase, or laptop carrying bag. Small drives can still have large capacities; the Iomega eGo Helium Portable hard drive can hold up to 1,280,000 photos. Smaller format drives are often bus powered, meaning that they get their power from the laptop, eliminating the need for an external power supply.

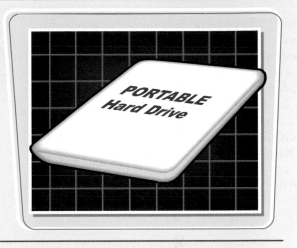

Picture Viewers

A picture viewer is a portable, battery-operated hard drive with a built-in viewer. You can insert memory cards to download, store, view, and print digital photographs independently from a computer. Some picture viewers such as the Picture Porter Elite (www.digitalfoci.com) can also function as an MP3 player and voice and video recorder.

Portable Photo Storage

Some portable photo-storage devices combine a memory card with a hard drive without a viewing screen. Portable storage devices such as the Photo Safe II (www.digitalfoci.com) can be used independently from a computer to download and store digital photographs. The Photo Safe II also acts as a card reader so that you can transfer your photographs to and from a computer.

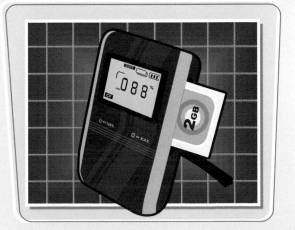

When traveling with your digital camera you should also take extra memory cards, multiple batteries and a battery charger, and a mini surge protector. You should also have two forms of hard drive storage and a card reader so that you can download images from memory cards while traveling.

Travel with a Laptop and Card Reader

A laptop and a card reader can enable you to download images to the hard drive. If iPhoto is installed on the laptop, you can even organize the downloaded photos within iPhoto while traveling. You should also travel with a small external drive so that you can make duplicates of your photos in case of a laptop hard drive failure. Make sure that the external drive is bus powered and that you pack the appropriate USB or FireWire cable and a mini surge protector.

Mini Travel Hard Drive

You can connect the card reader and the mini external drive to the laptop and transfer the contents of the memory card to the laptop and create duplicates on the external drive. If the laptop has iPhoto installed on it, you can import your photos with iPhoto by creating a single event or by dividing imported photos into separate events based on the date on which the photos were taken. See Chapter 2 for the steps to import photos from a digital camera into iPhoto.

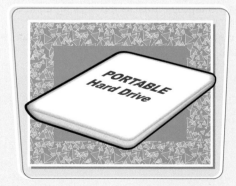

Multipurpose Travel Drive

Using a picture viewer, like the Picture Porter Elite, enables you to make copies of photos from the memory card and also copy them to a laptop. A picture viewer makes it easy for you to preview photos without turning on your laptop and even preview out to a television monitor.

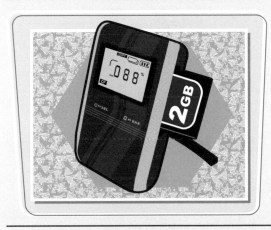

Portable Photo-Centric Hard Drive

A drive such as the Photo Safe II can function as a memory card reader to transfer photos from the memory card to a laptop, and as an external drive for downloading and storing images. A device such as this can be recharged by either a power adapter or by connecting to a computer with a USB cable.

Traveling Without a Laptop

You need to have backup storage capability while traveling. If you are going on the road without a laptop, consider purchasing a picture viewer and a second photo storage device. This way you will always have copies of your photos.

Index

Index

Index